The Rocking Chair Reader

Memories from the Attic

True Stories of Family Treasures Lost and Found

Edited by Helen Kay Polaski

Adams Media
Avon, Massachusetts

Published by
Adams Media, an F+W Publications Company
57 Littlefield Street, Avon, MA 02322. U.S.A.
www.adamsmedia.com and *www.rockingchairreader.com*

ISBN: 1-59337-270-1

Printed in the United States of America.

J I H G F E D C B A

Library of Congress Cataloging-in-Publication Data
Rocking chair reader : memories from the attic / edited by Helen Kay Polaski.
p.   cm.
ISBN 1-59337-270-1
1. United States—Social life and customs—Anecdotes. 2. Souvenirs
(Keepsakes)—United States—Anecdotes. 3. Heirlooms—United States—
Anecdotes. 4. United States—History, Local—Anecdotes. 5. United
States—Biography—Anecdotes. I. Polaski, Helen Kay.
E161.R69 2005
976.4'753—dc22
2004026333

Interior illustrations by Roberta A. Ridolfi.
Interior textures copyright ©2002 Marlin Studios.

This book is available at quantity discounts for bulk purchases.
For information, call 1-800-872-5627.

This book is dedicated to

the "pack rats" of the world,

for it is their nostalgic personalities,

overflowing closets, dust-filled attics,

and deep-seated sentimentality

that has kept our heritage strong.

Contents

◄o►

v

Acknowledgments

First and foremost, I thank God for everything. He has given me so much in the past year: this book series, the wonderful friendships that have been formed while working on this book, and the opportunity to spread my wings just a little bit further with each successive project.

Much hard work and talent goes into creating a book such as *The Rocking Chair Reader,* and I did not do it alone, nor could I have done it alone. Without the input from each and every one of my authors, this book would not be possible. I feel grateful to have worked in the midst of such gifted individuals, and pleased to have helped and encouraged the budding authors in the bunch. I am proud to be part of this talented group and thank each of you from the bottom of my heart for your patience and understanding, and your loyalty. Because you chose to submit your work to *The Rocking Chair Reader,* I was able to read your incredible stories and get to know you on a more personal basis. For that I will always be grateful.

Thank you, also, to the dedicated individuals who helped organize the town profiles: Carol I. Brown, Cathy Christesson, M. DeLoris Henscheid, Loren Jost, Diane L. McCord, Mary McGuire,

Jim Mills, Helen Luecke, Bertha Hellmer, Christine Klingaman, Harriette Niemi, and Marlene Wisuri. Thank you so much for taking the time out of your busy schedules to help me uncover such interesting and intimate facts about your corner of the world. God willing, one day I will meet each of you in person.

I'd also like to extend a huge thank-you to the "Adams Girls" who worked so hard to make this book perfect in every aspect. Kate Epstein, Kirsten Amann, Bridget Brace, Kate McBride, and Meredith O'Hayre all deserve a great big round of applause. I also want to thank the behind-the-scenes workers, whom I have never met. Because I know that everyone at Adams Media takes an interest in each book they publish, I would like to extend a heartfelt thank-you to everyone for helping to make our book another Adams Media success.

I'd also like to thank my former editors and friends at *The Milan News-Leader*. Renee Collins showed me the ropes and then stuck around to make sure I didn't hang myself, Tom Kirvan believed in me, and Paul Tull gave my fledgling career wings. I will never forget the years we had together.

Last, but by far not least, I also would like to thank our readers. It is our hope that this second book in *The Rocking Chair Reader* series will find its way into your hearts and become one of your very own memories from the attic.

Introduction

I NEEDN'T LOOK AROUND MY HOME to realize that I'm surrounded by so many memories. I've always had a hard time parting with stuff. Sometimes my family rolls their eyes at me and I know they're thinking I should get rid of some of it, but I don't want to. The items, like my memories, are too valuable to me to ever be discarded.

There, on a shelf in the kitchen, is my grandmother's green Depression-era glass creamer. The same one my mother kept our milk money in when I was a child, and which my own children scooped their milk money from not so long ago. Those of us who have been a part of its history need only glance at it to be reminded of happy times.

The black-and-white office sign hanging above my pantry door is a reminder of my writing roots. The seventeen years I spent as a journalist/photographer for *The Milan News* went by swiftly, but will never be forgotten. The 1960s jukebox in my entryway is a nostalgic reminder of the three years I owned and operated Stella's 16 Flavors, an old-fashioned ice-cream parlor named after my mother and her sixteen children. The records—all forty-fives—are timeless treasures that will remain in my family forever.

I have everything—from the set of canisters my sister Veronica gave me for my wedding shower thirty years ago, to the bride-and-groom statue that plays the tune to *The Godfather* that my sister Pam purchased for my wedding cake, to a red tin with a round crystal handle that I chose as a memento from my grandmother's house the week she departed this world. I have blue Mason jars that remind me of learning to can tomatoes and peaches at my mother's side, and another jar with a wire handle that at one time held honey from my Uncle Martin's honeycombs, and later had its lid riddled with holes so we could catch lightning bugs in the balmy summer evenings and bumblebees as they buzzed about the lilac bush and hollyhocks each morning.

A Christmas card my mother penned to my family, many years before she was promoted to heaven, graces my wall every December along with current Christmas cards from family and friends. The delicate flowered hankies Mom always seemed to have in her possession can now be found in my purse and in the purses of other women in our family, but if that's not enough, I've got dozens of photos that keep my loved ones and our shared memories close to me despite the distance that separates us.

When I think of memories from the attic, I think of home. I think of my siblings and the joy we shared as we wandered through our childhood, growing older and presumably smarter each day as we carted our possessions with us from this spot to that, losing some in the process, but always creating memories that will forever be a part of who we are. As you read these stories, I know they'll prompt you to recall memories from your own childhood. And I know you'll smile because the recollections will be the special ones. You know—the ones that stay with you forever—the ones you would never discard.

Helen Kay Polaski

Beach Patrol

by Candy Killion | *Cape May, New Jersey*

LIKE MILLIONS OF OTHERS, I love the ocean and everything connected to it, and am fortunate enough to live close by, at the southern
end of Florida—where the weather is balmy and the water pristine,
year-round. But, my fifty-year love affair with the Atlantic didn't
start here in the tropics; I became enamored of the feel of gritty sand
between my toes and the smell of salt in my hair decades back and
more than a thousand miles away, in New Jersey.

I'd almost forgotten how the sea had been washed into my soul
until recently, when I came across an old black-and-white Brownie
snapshot at the bottom of a box of family photos. In the picture, a
chunky, solidly built girl of about four, round-faced and sporting one
of those old Campbell Kids haircuts—dark brown bangs cut straight
across—stood alone on a beach, flanked by a lifeguard dinghy marked
CAPE MAY BEACH PATROL.

The picture wasn't like the ones you can pluck easily from anyone's seashore collection, where families ham it up for the camera
and make-believe captains scamper on the decks of safely grounded
craft, waving for posterity. In this photo, the child was oblivious

to the photographer, chubby legs planted solidly into sand and tanned pudgy arms flung backward. Her attention was focused on the sea—her upturned face jubilant, the ocean air buffeting her hair westward.

She looked as though she was about to get a running start for the ocean's edge, and the look on her face promised that nothing would get in her way. I know this is true, because the child in the photo is me.

I was a city kid back in the 1950s, hop-scotching the sooty slate sidewalks of Down Neck, Newark, for most of the year, but come summer, my father loaded us into his sky-blue '52 Plymouth and headed for Route 9—and for two months I was not a city kid. Route 9 was not at all like the state-of-the-art and speedier Garden State Parkway that opened for traffic in '54, where the urbanites swore under their breath at having to feed the newfangled tollbooth coin catchers, but it left a lasting impression of its own. Daddy liked to take the long way, seventy miles or so down the old, pitted two-lane through sleepy bog towns with names like Tuckerton, where an old rocking chair sat weathered atop the widow's watch of a peeling Victorian, facing the east toward the churning surf.

This photo was taken during the summer of '58 and I remember it well. Cape May: the seaside town at the southernmost tip of New Jersey, where time stood still, adopted me, welcoming me back every time . . . wrapping me in its small-town arms.

The Cape is surrounded by water: the Atlantic to the east, the Tuckahoe River to the north, the mighty Delaware Bay to the west. Bluefish and stripers all but leapt from the waves to our lines, and on the days my father sought out yet another secluded freshwater pond, crappie seemed everywhere. Frogs and turtles became my best friends, the diamondback terrapins my favorite of all, since they were gutsy enough to plant one slow-moving foot in front of the other at any given time, crossing the highway to the salt marsh, ignoring the blaring tourist horns. The terrapins set the pace for lazy summer days at Cape May—where nothing was hurried—against the backdrop of gingerbread Victorians painted in pinks and purples and Wedgwood blues, sporting polished mahogany front doors and sparkling stained-glass windows. Turrets and countless widow's walks pierced skies that seemed almost painfully blue and beautiful. But still, my favorite place then—and now—was the beach. Milky quartz dotted the Cape May sand, glistening like diamonds. White, powdery dunes nearly as high as me, some higher, spread parallel to the water as far as I could see, beach grass whispering and waving among them. And ahead, the surf.

Nearly out to the curve of the horizon, if you looked hard enough, the arc of a leaping dolphin could be seen. I stood by the dinghy, squinted, and made out the shape of one, dancing and leaping, dancing and leaping again. I threw back my head and my arms and laughed, ready to rush toward the water, to dance and leap along with the dolphins.

And that was when my father clicked the lens of the Brownie, saving my Cape May moment. For me, it is a reminder that the ever-constant sea lives and flows, and it ties me to it, the terrapins, and the diamonds in the dunes. ೧ು

The Perfect Place

by Helen Luecke | *Memphis, Texas*

RECENTLY, WHILE CLEANING OUT A CLOSET, I came across an old, coverless softball. Kids today would throw it away. I clutched it to my chest and smiled, and my mind raced back to carefree, fun-filled days in the small town of Memphis, Texas. The year was 1946. It was the perfect place, the perfect time, and I had the perfect Daddy.

Everyone who knew him called him "Shack," but to me he was Daddy. He stood 5'7" and weighed 155 pounds. He had sky blue eyes and a balding head.

"Why do people call you Shack?" I asked as we walked to the corner lot for our daily softball game.

"It's a nickname for Shackelford," he said. Satisfied, I grabbed his hand and skipped along.

As we passed the Newmans' house, Daddy stopped, pushed back his worn straw hat, and let out a whistle. "Would you look at that new car—a 1946 Ford." He ran his hand lightly across the shiny black fender.

"Come on, Daddy. It's my turn to choose a team," I urged, pulling him away from the vehicle. Daddy took one more wishful look before making his way to the vacant lot that was filling up with neighborhood kids.

Joyce and I selected teams. I let her pick Babs—because who would want her sister on the same team?

"We're ready," I yelled to Daddy, who served as umpire, scorekeeper, and peacemaker.

"Just a minute," Daddy said. He turned to a skinny boy standing next to the old elm tree.

"Come on over here, son," I heard him say. "We have room on Cozy's team for another player."

I tugged at his pant leg and whispered, "Bobby can't play ball."

"Nonsense," Daddy said. His blue eyes blazed as he gave me his "Be quiet" look.

"I-I'm not very good, sir," Bobby stammered, his pale face turning bright red.

"Sure you are," Daddy said. Then he patted Bobby's shoulder and added, "You can if you think you can. All it takes is practice."

My team lost. Bobby struck out twice and missed a fly ball. After Babs and I had gathered the cracked bats and the coverless ball and started home, I glanced back at Daddy. He stood at home plate talking to Bobby.

"Boy, we sure beat y'all good," Babs teased.

Tears burned my eyes. "You know why, don't you? Bobby was on our team."

Babs grinned, enjoying the moment. "Admit it Cozy, you got beat. And you didn't play so good yourself."

"Oh yeah!" I hollered. "I caught a fly ball, and look at this." I pointed to my skinned and bloody knee.

"It's just a game," Babs said as she twirled the bat like a baton and hummed "Take Me Out to the Ball Game."

When we got home, I sat on the porch, staring at my banged-up knee and feeling sorry for myself.

In the fading light, Daddy entered the yard and sat down in a lawn chair next to me. "Come here, Cozy," he said, patting his knee. I crawled onto his lap, sure he was going to tell me that I was right, that Bobby really couldn't play ball.

"How old are you, Cozy?"

Startled, I answered, "You know I'm seven. Why?"

"How long have you played softball?"

"Forever, I guess."

"That's right, Cozy, since you first started walking and running around. But I guess you've forgotten how many times you went into the house crying because you couldn't hit the ball."

A sickness filled my stomach. Yes, I remembered those times, and I also remembered Daddy's words: "Cozy, you can do anything you set your mind to. Just remember, you can if you think you can."

Knowing immediately where the conversation was going, I buried my face in Daddy's khaki shirt and let the tears roll. "I was mean to Bobby, wasn't I?"

"Yes, you were." He rocked me in his arms slowly, then said, "Treat others the way that you want them to treat you."

"I'm sorry, Daddy," I sputtered as I struggled to wipe my eyes in the big white handkerchief he handed me.

"Bobby is the one who needs the apology."

I wiped my nose, then shook my head quickly. "No, I couldn't."

We sat in the darkness and listened to the crickets and the distant whistle of a train.

Finally Daddy spoke. "Bobby doesn't have a father. He was killed in the war."

"The war Uncle James was in?"

Daddy nodded. "Bobby never had anyone to teach him how to play. With time and practice he'll be one fine player." He smoothed my rumpled hair. "Cozy, winning isn't everything. Just remember, there's always someone better than you."

I wasn't in the mood for Daddy's words of wisdom. My knee throbbed and I had a big old knot in my stomach that tightened with each breath. It was the kind of knot that you get when you've done something wrong and you know that it won't go away until you right it.

Daddy picked me up and carried me into the house. "Those two homers were good hits."

I hugged his neck and whispered, "Tomorrow I'll tell Bobby I'm sorry."

"I knew you would. Now let's go doctor your knee."

Soon, Bobby had become the best player around.

Early one fall morning, Bobby called to me as I came out of class. "Cozy, would you do something for me?"

"If you'll choose me first when it's your turn to be captain," I quipped.

His face turned serious. "My mother remarried and we're moving. I won't see Shack again, so would you tell him thanks for me?"

"What for?"

"Just tell him, 'you can if you think you can,' and he'll understand."

As I watched Bobby turn and run across the playground to a waiting car, I realized I did understand. ⤖

Memphis, Texas

Population: 3,800

Famous Folks

Hall County is named after Warren D. C. Hall, who was secretary of war while Texas was a Republic.

U.S. Congressman Jack Hightower was born in Memphis.

Actor Tommy Lee Jones's father, Clyde C. Jones, was born in Memphis.

Boxcar Willie's mother, Edna Jones Marlin, lived in Memphis.

Bob Wills and his Texas Playboys lived in nearby Turkey, Texas, and played in Memphis. The Bob Wills Museum is a short drive from Memphis, and is a must-see if you're in the neighborhood.

Elsie Bass Guthrie, a local teacher who taught junior and senior English in Memphis High School, was named "Top Teacher in Texas" in 1964 and listed among the Ten Best Teachers in the United States. At the age of seventy-six, she wrote a novel titled *The Lucky Moores.*

Train Tales

*B*ecause Memphis was without a depot in its early day, trains did not stop in the village. Certain citizens sought to remedy that situation by smearing the tracks with lye soap, and before long, an agreement was struck between town promoters and the railroad officials. In 1891, a depot was built and businesses were moved on wheels from Salisbury to the new county seat, where a courthouse of homemade bricks was constructed in 1892. ❧

Town Facts

First incorporated • Memphis was first incorporated on June 18, 1906. The village was without a name for a time, and as the story goes, Reverend Brice, while in Austin, happened to see a letter addressed to Memphis, Texas, rather than Memphis, Tennessee. The letter had the notation "no such town in Texas" written on it. Reverend Brice thought about it a spell, and the name was submitted to and accepted by the powers that be.

Transportation • The railroad was a popular mode of transportation in the late 1890s.

Location • Memphis, the county seat of Hall County, is at the junction of US Highway 287, State Highway 256, and Farm Road 1547, in the northeastern part of the county. It is sixty-four miles southeast of Amarillo, twenty-eight miles southeast of Clarendon, and twenty-nine miles northeast of Childress.

Places of note • The Hall County Historical Museum, an interesting place to spend an afternoon looking through the past, is located on the Square at 6th and Main. The Presbyterian Building, formerly a church designed after St. Peter's Cathedral in Rome, contains one of only two rare pipe organs of its type remaining in the United States. The Old Historical Memphis Hotel, which opened October 12, 1926, currently is a popular area bed-and-breakfast.

Local attractions • In 1935, E. M. Ewen and his wife formed the Hall County Old Settlers Reunion, now called the Hall County Picnic Association. The association holds a two-day celebration each September, and now features a rodeo as part of the festivities.

Fifty blocks of city streets were paved in 1926 and remain in use today. Memphis is also noted for its tree-lined streets, two swimming pools, a community center, and a large city park—ideal for family reunions.

Industry • The annual Cotton Boll Enduro, a 125-mile cross-country motorcycle event held in October, begins and ends in Memphis. Cotton was and still is Memphis's main crop. In 1973, and again in 1979, Hall County gins turned out more than 100,000 bales of cotton. No wonder Memphis's logo reads, "Memphis, Cotton Capital of the Panhandle."

A Mother's Gift

by Lisa Ciriello | *Lawton, Oklahoma*

ONE OF MY EARLIEST CHILDHOOD MEMORIES of growing up in Lawton, Oklahoma, is of playing "bride," standing before the full-length mirror in my parents' bedroom, swathed in a white bedsheet with a lace tablecloth covering my head. I'd look up at the picture on my mother's dresser, transfixed by the image of her in her wedding gown, dancing with my father. Captured in that moment, she was, and still is, the happiest and most beautiful woman I've ever seen.

Over the years, my mother's wedding gown became a symbol to me of love, security, and hope. It was originally worn by my great-grandmother, passed down to my grandmother, and finally to my mother. It has since been carefully preserved and stored in the attic of my parents' home, lying in wait for the next hopeful bride. The gown itself is unadorned ivory silk with a full A-line skirt, long sleeves, and a modest scoop neckline. It is a simple, timeless design that is just as stylish now as it was when my great-grandmother donned it for the first time.

At the age of ten or eleven, I remember begging my mother to show me the gown in the picture. I wanted to touch the smooth fabric, feel its smoothness against my cheek, and imagine myself wearing it someday at my own wedding. An annual ritual was born from my request that day.

Each year after that, on my parents' wedding anniversary, my mother and I climbed the attic stairs together.

Every time she lifted the cover and removed the gown from the box, I was overcome with a sense of awe and reverence for the history that this garment represented. Three generations of women wore this very gown on the first day of their married lives; their excitement, anticipation, and hopefulness were woven within its very fibers.

I've since moved out on my own and the ritual my mother and I shared died with her. It had been five years since we climbed those attic steps and I fingered the silky fabric as I listened to wedding stories about the women who came before me.

On the evening my fiancé and I announced our engagement, my father motioned me away from our family and friends and led me to the attic stairs. We made our way to that familiar corner of the attic, where he presented me with a large box wrapped in silver paper. I didn't need to unwrap it to know what it contained.

We didn't say a word, but the smile on my father's face, and the sweet sadness in his eyes, told me that he felt my mother's presence as strongly as I did that night. With his help, she was there to pass on a time-honored tradition within our family.

As I imagine my trip down the aisle next year, I think about the future—the life my new husband and I will create together, the children we hope to bring into the world, the goals we share coming to fruition, the new traditions we'll create, and the existing ones we'll continue. It's impossible to think about the future, however, without also contemplating the past—the tradition of love shared by three generations of brides who have preceded me, manifested within the beautiful silk gown that I'll be wearing on that day. ☜

Church House Mouse

by Rollie Barton | *O'Fallon, Illinois*

I DID NOT EXPECT O'FALLON, ILLINOIS, to be the same. Sixty-five years can sponsor a dramatic makeover—a McDonald's restaurant was built over the spot where my brothers and I had played marbles. The farm beside Highway 50, across from where my dad's Texaco service station had been, now sported stores, parking lots, warehouses, and merchant activity. There was a sort of plastic sheen over everything I had stockpiled in my mind as genuine. On that farm I had walked, by the hour, behind Hidorn's horse-drawn plow as it turned the rich soil, pleasured by the cool earth on my bare feet as I trudged along in the bottom of the continuous furrow our combined effort created.

All of the hitching posts were gone, but the railroad tracks still bisected what had been the old town I knew, and there were remnants of old buildings standing, which I'd walked past as a teenager. A few blocks across the tracks, I expected to see our old church, but it was gone; it had burned to the ground many years ago. That church was the hub of our existence, the place for social activity, for spiritual instruction, and for the pursuit of truth.

One summer, the men and boys dug a basement under the church. Somehow the substantial building was supported while we dug, by hand, a basement cavity under the whole structure. We labored like pit mules under there. We filled buckets, containers, and wheelbarrows with the dirt and carted it away. (OSHA would have shut us down in a minute.) To my young mind, it seemed impossible to finish, but we did, and the finished product more than doubled the utility of the church.

We attended that old church every Sunday, morning and evening, or any time the doors were open. There were no locks, so it was open all the time. The church, for the most part, was worship and solemnity, but there was a mix of activities—potlucks, ice-cream socials, Christmas plays, Thanksgiving feasts—and sometimes an unplanned experience got embedded in our memory banks.

⌒∾⌒

My family sat together in church primarily because we were ordered to do so. There must have been some merit in it because the preacher always commented on how nice it was to see such a wonderfully close-knit family worshipping together. My two brothers and I tried to keep Mother or Aunt Min between Dad and us, in case we were caught playing tic-tac-toe, giggling at scribbled notes, or riffling the pages of the hymnal. Not that we could escape punishment in any case, but Dad used the most stringent measures to command reverence. The few moments we forfeited to reverence were a high price to pay for the inactive games a church pew provides. Playing around during the services was a risky business that had to be weighed against the dullness of a droning monotone pitched to adult ears. Our folks always seemed to get the sense out of the preacher's words, and yet kept a complete tally of what we did before drowsiness slipped over us.

The sedation of a lofty sermon was little protection from Aunt Min's elbow as it entered the ribs of the closest kid with all the fleshiness of a sheathed bayonet. She objected to heavy, openmouthed breathing, for which all three of us could have been convicted at one time or another. Despite this, Aunt Min was a showpiece of decorum, especially in church. She looked straight at the preacher, her head high and prim as though intent on his every word. We always swore she sneezed in her stomach; not a sound would escape her spare frame. The hanky she carried probably never met a full-blown crisis head on; she dabbed at her nose occasionally with it or pulled it nervously through her fingers in a way that featured her timidity. This quality in her numbered the days when she could control three restless boys in church.

Our church was one of those Midwestern, steepled types with a roof that would split a raindrop. It had long, skinny, subdivided windows; pews designed for square people; a bell that we tried many times to turn over; and a balcony from which a kid could see everything that went on yet still feel hidden by the open rail in front of it, that is, if he was ever allowed up there. Upstairs or down, the floor under the austere furnishings tattled on every movement you made during any solemn occasion.

One fateful day, my little brother was next to Aunt Min; the sermon was half-spent and sleep had more appeal for us than foolishness. A mouse suddenly appeared between the pews in front of us; he was walking by as casual as could be. I don't know how he got by all the folks behind us unless the parson had a grip on everyone else. Anyway, it rescued the whole evening. My brother poked a toe at the mouse's tail real easylike and he must have touched it because the mouse turned and ducked for cover—right up Aunt Min's leg, as fast as he could go. For not knowing there was such a creature around, her instinctive reactions were amazing. Quick as a cat, with hanky in hand, she apprehended the little beast alongside her right knee together with a wad of dress. A noise like a hiss in reverse escaped her clenched teeth as she squeezed hard and locked her elbow straight-armed, yet to all outward appearances was still serene and loyal to the sanctity of the moment.

We appreciated all of the fun and none of her terror. The beginnings of a snicker from three boys brought a glare from Dad, which squelched audible laughter and drove it convulsively down our insides. I believe he would have laughed, himself, had he known.

Poor Aunt Min sat with the devil in hand without flinching for about a half hour, while we suffered with stillborn laughter. The preacher appended the "amen" to the benedictions, and it triggered a dammed-up scream you could have heard at the Methodist church a block away. Up she jumped, knocking the little creature out of her dress as she leaped aside; the mouse thudded to the worn floor, quite dead.

Although emotionally expensive for Aunt Min, and exorbitantly costly for the mouse, I think the price was right. Entirely unsupported by the preacher's text, that poor little church mouse laid bare a salient truth: Never fall asleep in church—you might miss something. ᕰ

Buttons and Clover

by Cheryl D. Stauffer | *Chilton, Wisconsin*

ONE SUMMER, A SCABBY-KNEED LITTLE GIRL with stringy hair sat beside an old woman scouring the clover patch on the front lawn for four-leaf clovers. They had already had a good outing, as anyone could tell by the pile lying beside them.

I was that little girl. My grandmother and I shared an uncanny ability to find four-leaf clovers instantly, in any clover patch. I lived in Georgia, but each summer I made the trip to Chilton, Wisconsin, to spend the summer with Grandma. Chilton was where my mother grew up and where everyone either knew Grandma or was related to her.

The farm had a two-story house with a full basement. From this basement, my grandmother ran a perpetual rummage sale. Each morning, she'd put the RUMMAGE SALE AND DEHYDRATORS FOR SALE sign out by the road, and every day, people stopped.

Grandma always invited her rummage sale customers into the kitchen to sit down at the table and taste this or that, while talking about the weather, health, and how our families were. It was a rarity to have a customer leave before the hour was up. People felt comfortable with Grandma and enjoyed the time talking together, and they always left the rummage sale with something—a trinket perhaps, maybe a book, or a free sample package of Grandma's dehydrated soup mix.

The soup mix was full of good stuff: onions, carrots, celery, and seasonings, all sealed in a plastic sandwich bag. Grandma was always concocting recipes for the dehydrators she sold. In fact, Grandma dried anything she could put on dehydrator trays—even meat! Over the years, the local paper wrote several stories about her enterprises. In Chilton, a town of 2,965, Grandma was an icon.

In between rummage-sale customers, my grandmother had many ways to keep busy. She was a gatherer; anything she could find—flowers, herbs, vegetables—she'd figure out a way to make it into something useful. I spent many hours at the foot of her ladder talking to her as she picked blossoms off the linden tree while the competing honeybees buzzed around her head.

But my very favorite pastime was when she brought out the five-gallon jars full of buttons she had saved over the years. She had grown up during the Depression and retained that pack-rat mentality so common to people of that era. She saved everything. There was a narrow path that wound through her house . . . to her bed . . . the window . . . and the closet. The rest of the room was packed so tightly you could go no farther. But the button jars were in the closet and we always managed to get to them when I visited. That's how we always began our visit, with my snatching buttons by the fistful. I loved the *click-clack* sounds they made as I dropped them slowly back into their containers. After the initial button-grabbing frenzy, I would set about sorting the buttons, trying to match all the button families together.

As we sat there at her kitchen table and sorted buttons together, she talked about her childhood. She told me the story of how her mother had died when she was a young woman. Since my grandmother was the eldest of six, she quit school and stayed home to help her father take care of her brothers and sisters. She was in love, but the love of her life had to wait seven years to marry her because she felt she needed to wait until her siblings were old enough to care for themselves. She and her "Eddie" had a mere seven years together before he was taken from her in a car crash that left her a widow with a dairy farm, a crushed knee, and three small children. Her six-year-old son went through the windshield, and my mother, at age two, broke both her legs and her collarbone. Grandma never remarried or even hinted at being interested. She always talked about missing her "Eddie." We sorted buttons together at least once during every trip to Chilton.

When it was time to leave, I would cry for days. To ease the pain of leaving Chilton, Grandma and I mailed four-leaf clovers to each other to remind us of the time we shared while I was with her, and to confirm that we would do it again. One time she sent me a sheet of 100 four-leaf clovers that she had found, pressed, and glued to a piece of paper. This went on until I finished high school.

When Grandma died, my mom, aunt, uncle, cousins, and I spent the day before her funeral going through her room. We found boxes upon boxes of useless stuff—jars of elastic scraps, a small box of rocks (labeled "from my daughter's house in Georgia"), an olive twig from the garden of Gethsemane, and other things that made sense only to her.

And the buttons. I immediately gathered up all the jars of buttons I could find. I opened jar after jar, letting them *click-clack* through my hands once again. In the midst of all those buttons, I found two small buttons shaped like four-leaf clovers. Memories of finding four-leaf clovers with my grandmother surfaced and I quickly put the two buttons into my pocket for safekeeping.

The next morning, I put the two buttons in the pocket of my dress and walked out the door, on my way to Grandma's funeral. As I stood by the open casket greeting family and friends, I reached into my pocket and stroked the buttons, taking comfort in the link that Grandma and I shared. Then, just before the service was to begin, I said my final prayer and tucked one of the small buttons in with Grandma.

When I returned to Georgia, I tenderly placed the last four-leaf clover Grandma and I would ever exchange into my jewelry box. These days, whenever I need Grandma by my side, I open the jewelry box and hold the four-leaf clover button in my hand, and I feel her with me once again. ᔕ

The Auction

by Jim James | *Riverton, Wyoming*

ONE COLD MORNING LAST WINTER, I sat in my favorite reading chair with a cup of hot coffee, watching the Wyoming snow fall. My gaze took me much farther than my front yard that snowy day. It took me all the way back to the day I acquired the chair I was sitting in, the day I learned a valuable lesson about living in small-town Wyoming.

I was born and raised in Los Angeles, but when I was thirty-five, I left California and moved to Wyoming, the "Cowboy State." My parents had met and married on a farm in Madison County, Iowa, and had tried to give my sister and me a feel for small-town values, but growing up in Southern California did nothing to enhance what they wanted us to appreciate. Moving to Wyoming was serious culture shock for me, but I thought I'd stick it out.

I was living in Riverton, an agriculture and ranching town, with a population of about 5,000, and had made the acquaintance of Charlie, a local rancher. He owned a small ranch on the Wind River and had a reputation for being a good businessman.

I walked into Charlie's kitchen one Saturday morning, looking for the coffeepot, and he asked if I wanted to go to a ranch auction. I said, "Sure." I'd never been to an auction, let alone one on a ranch. We filled our coffee mugs, the ones with his brand stamped on the side, and climbed into his well-used pickup.

On the drive out to the ranch, I had visions of purchasing a couple of antiques, maybe some ranch equipment at bargain-basement prices. I really didn't need anything, but what the heck, a bargain is a bargain.

We drove the few miles to the homestead where a crowd slowly collected, pickups parked willy-nilly in the drive and on the lawn under the cottonwood trees. Charlie parked his truck likewise, and we got out. We wandered around the grounds, looking at the stuff for sale, Charlie introducing me to most of the people we ran into. There was lots of socializing and it seemed to me that everyone knew everyone else. I found an old chair needing reupholstering, but with a good hardwood frame. I figured if I could get it for five or ten bucks, I'd go to the extra expense of having it restored.

Near noon, the auctioneer, speaking through a cardboard megaphone, announced the order that the items would be sold. "We'll start on the lawn," he said, "do the gardening equipment, go into the house and do the furniture, then to the corrals and do the livestock and ranch equipment. The tractor and the backhoe will be last, so you guys out here for the big machines, go get a beer and come back about three o'clock."

That was all he said before the bidding started. The congregation ebbed and flowed behind the auctioneer, the front of the crowd interlacing back and forth, like square dancers, depending on the interest in the item up for bid.

The first piece was a rusty old lawnmower with a gasoline engine, worth maybe twenty dollars. Bidding started slowly, in increments of one dollar on up to five. Charlie jumped in when the bidding hit forty bucks. I might have been from the city, but I had priced power lawnmowers a few weeks before, and a decent one, brand new, would go for about eighty-nine dollars at the Western Auto store. Charlie ended up getting this one for eighty dollars! I didn't say anything out loud, but I sure wondered what had happened to Charlie's good business sense.

Nothing appealed to me until an antique dresser came up for bid. Then I moved to the front of the crowd, figuring it was worth fifty dollars, maybe seventy-five. It appeared to be in good shape, had a very nice beveled mirror, and the finish was excellent. Before I knew it, the bidding had surpassed $100 and was still going up in increments of ten dollars with every bid. It sold for $220—way more than it was worth.

Next was the bed. It was a four-poster and would obviously need a new mattress, but as far as I could see, the frame was worth up to $200. I was amazed when someone paid 380 hard-earned dollars for it.

I tapped Charlie on the shoulder and whispered, "Those things are worth nowhere near those prices. And *you* could've bought a brand-new lawnmower for less than you paid for that rusty old thing out in the yard."

Charlie didn't say a word. Instead, he tipped his head to the side, motioning me to follow him. We worked our way back through the crowd in the house, going out the kitchen door to the backyard. Charlie maintained his silence as he led me toward a large cottonwood tree where an old man sat alone in the shade. As we approached, the man glanced up, his old rocking chair slowly moving back and forth, barely disturbing the coffee in the cup he held in his hand. I couldn't help but notice how threadbare his faded bib overalls were, and how his cowboy hat resembled something that ordinarily would be used to start a campfire. As we approached, his well-lined face, the product of years in the Wyoming sun, was devoid of emotion.

"Jim, this is Wendell," Charlie said. Looking up at me sharply, as if the point he was trying to make was one I was supposed to have already figured out, he added, "Wendell's wife died a year ago and he has to sell out." As the words left Charlie's mouth, he reached out and put his hand on Wendell's shoulder and squeezed gently. "Wendell, this is Jim. He's from California." Charlie's last statement sounded like an accusation.

Wendell stuck out his hand and we shook, his grip weak and shaky, his bony fingers pressing against mine. Wendell looked at me kindly but said nothing. I still didn't understand what Charlie was trying to tell me, so I looked up at him questioningly.

Charlie patted Wendell on the shoulder and turned, walking back toward the auction. I nodded to Wendell, and he nodded back at me.

When I finally caught up with Charlie, he kept his eyes focused straight ahead while he explained the situation to the dimwit walking at his side. "Jim," he said slowly, "we really don't care what this stuff is worth. Wendell is our neighbor and our friend. And he needs the money."

Culture shock.

The $10 chair I had seen? I paid $100 for it. As I picked it up to put it in Charlie's pickup, I felt as if I had finally figured out what life in Wyoming is all about. I had the chair reupholstered and still sit in it today. It's my favorite reading chair, the best bargain I ever got. ⌣

THE TOWN OF

Riverton, Wyoming

Population: 10,050

Annual Attractions

*R*iverton is home to an annual "mountain man" rendezvous, held during the first week of July, on the site of the
original 1838 Fur Trappers' and Traders' Rendezvous.

The town also boasts more yearly reasons to celebrate: the
Wild West Winter Carnival (February); Cinco de Mayo Fiesta
(May); various powwows (June through September); and the Fre-
mont County Fair and Rodeo (August). Riverton celebrates its
centennial year in 2006. ∾

Local Arts

*R*iverton resident Ron Staker has entered his paintings in
the Wyoming Conservation Stamp Art contest every
year since 1986, placing second three times, fourth once, and receiving one honorable mention. His painting titled "A Burrowing
Afternoon" was chosen as the winner of the 2005 award and appears on the ten-dollar conservation stamp Wyoming hunters and
anglers are required to purchase each year. Staker has also entered
similar contests in Colorado, Nevada, and Oregon, and in 1995,
he finished first in the Utah upland game stamp contest with his
rendition of a Gambel's quail. ∾

Town Facts

First incorporated • Riverton was founded on August 15, 1906. The individuals who settled the area were firm believers in the idea that the West offered opportunities not available in other parts of the country and saw themselves as part of the pioneering movement that had begun decades earlier.

Transportation • Riverton is served by a commuter airline that provides several roundtrip flights daily to Denver, Colorado, but most visitors arrive by private automobile.

Location • Riverton, adjacent to the Wind River Indian Reservation—home of the Eastern Shoshone and the Northern Arapaho tribes—is the leading commercial city in west-central Wyoming. It is a five-hour drive from Riverton to Salt Lake City, Denver, and Billings, Montana.

Places of note • The area is surrounded by mountains and rivers. Tucked in between the Wind River Range of the Rocky Mountains on the west, the Owl Creek Range on the north, the Gas Hills and Wind River to the east, and the Little Wind River and South Pass to the south, Riverton experiences a mild climate with more than 340 sunny days, on average. Additionally, Riverton has several important prehistoric rock art sites, not to be missed.

Industry • In the 1950s, uranium deposits were discovered nearby. Though the town experienced a mining boom from 1950 through 1970, the mineral was depleted by the 1980s and the mines were closed. Other than during those boom mining years, Riverton's economy has depended on its rich soil for farming and ranching. Snow falls mainly in the mountains, but a series of strategically located irrigation canals brings the runoff to the crops below, helping to keep Riverton's agriculture a thriving business.

The Spirit of the Journey

by Charles Perry | *Belen, New Mexico*

THE COOL BREEZES OF AUTUMN amused themselves with soft wind squalls, slowly scattering the curled, fading leaves. A wisp of wind, then another, and a leaf fell gently to the ground. As I watched from my window, reflecting upon a less-than-stellar year, I saw Belen, New Mexico, turn from summer to fall and heard myself whisper, "It's almost over." Fall, always a favorite time, was both peaceful and forgiving.

As I continued to watch, a familiar flash of red bolted up the street: Maggie's old red truck. Though Maggie usually went next door to my sister's, today I met her on the porch and invited her in. We sat at the table, uncomfortable at first, with little conversation. I tried cranking up my joking side, but no one seemed amused, and she quickly changed the subject and asked what I had been doing lately. I answered that I hadn't been doing anything, just resigned to little work and feeling like a slug. Suddenly, she smiled, said she wanted to check the Romero Ranch, and asked me to ride along. For some reason, she didn't want to go alone this time.

"They were originally brought from Spain," she said, and I knew she was referring to the wild horses that roamed the ranch. It really didn't make any difference to me if they were original descendants of the Spanish Barbs, purebred in nature, and ancestors of those Iberian horses, specially bred for war.

"Have you ever been to the ranch?" she asked.

I nodded, vaguely remembering one visit when I had taken a picture of the very old-looking bunkhouse. History had always interested me, and that old adobe house near the corral looked as if it had come straight off of a movie set. I grabbed my camera and a roll of film and we were off. It might be fun to photograph the horses and I certainly would want to photograph the buildings.

Within an hour, we were bouncing around the hills, Maggie explaining the significance of the Spanish Barb history to me while driving through gullies and riverbeds—my head hitting the ceiling over and over. It didn't take long before my head was battered and my hat mashed on one side.

The countryside looked depleted. Grayish yellow grass stuck straight up from the ground, dry and brittle. The Romero Ranch house, deserted for years, blended in with the landscape, as if it had been there forever. Wandering the grounds, I checked for arrowheads and Spanish coins and took photographs of the building from all angles. Then we got back into the cab and were off again.

"The wild horses hide in the junipers, those gnarled trees that look dead," Maggie said pointing excitedly, despite my lack of interest. But when I looked where she pointed, it was my turn to be excited. The magnificent beasts showed themselves, and I was immediately sorry I had only one roll of film.

"Let me set up my tripod in the back, Maggie."

We moved down the old path slowly. Maggie had done this before and knew just how to keep the horses from bolting. Several mares and a stallion watched with wide eyes, cautious and alert, keeping a safe distance. One of the mares was beautiful, unlike any horse I had ever seen. She was dark brown, almost black, with a silvery gold mane and a like-colored broom tail. In the hushed silence, I whispered, "If I had a place for her, that would be the one I would get." Maggie chuckled, wanting to know how I was planning on *getting* her.

In the distance, another group of horses appeared, walking single file around the base of the hill, while several stallions, nostrils flaring, stood statuesque, watching us. Snorting threats went ignored as we continued our perusal of the breathtaking beauty before us.

The bouncing of the truck continued as we rounded the hill and Maggie tapped lightly on the back window, signaling more horses, and then stopped the vehicle. Not fifty feet away, grazing with an unconcerned glance in our direction, was a band of five—maybe six—horses.

The wind blew gently as I prepared my camera, then slowly snapped the shutter. As if they knew what I wanted, the horses moved into position. I was changing from verticals to horizontals, my spine a superhighway of adrenaline. I wasn't myself. The excitement of seeing them in the wild like this was overwhelming. The horses teased, walking and running, stopping and looking at us, tossing their heads in the air to get our scent. Then they trotted over the hill, leaving me alone with my camera, out of film, spiritually and emotionally drained.

But there were more. From the other side of the road, six more stood majestically, even closer than the others had been, and I gripped my camera, now out of film, and could only watch as the opportunity of a lifetime passed. The old saying "I shall return" went through my mind at that moment. And many times since, I have returned, though without the initial thrill I felt that day with Maggie.

I often pick up those pictures of the historic Romero place and remember. No one lives there today, but a rich past lingers. Today's treasure is yesterday's whisper, a silent reminder of a time gone by, and of the horses, wild and free, still alive and older, maybe, than the Romero Ranch.

Dear Daddy

by Sandy Williams Driver | *Albertville, Alabama*

DEAR DADDY,

I wanted to write and tell you that I know about your hand. I'm sorry if you're mad at me for digging up the past, but I just had to find out. Growing up, I begged so many times for you to tell me how you lost two fingers and your left hand became so mangled. But you never answered. You just looked away with vacant eyes.

While everyone seemed to know what was going on in everyone else's life in our small hometown of Albertville, Alabama, not many people dared ask you directly about your accident. I could see the questions in their eyes, but your firm jaw line and deep voice deterred many from inquiring. You were just that sort of man. Even as you got older and a little frail, your presence demanded respect.

Momma didn't even know what had happened to your hand. Because of those disability checks from the government that arrived in the mail every month, she knew the injury had occurred while you were in the military.

Don't be angry, but I found a box of your things in the attic after you left. Inside were lots of official documents and a few photographs of you in a brand-new uniform. Your face was smooth and your blue eyes clear. You looked so young. A yellowed piece of paper dated October 12, 1945, had the words HONORABLE DISCHARGE written on one side and some information typed on the other.

I showed them to Momma and she said I could have them, so I took my treasure home and typed your unit number into the search engine of my computer. The 475th Infantry arrived in exotic India in the fall of 1944. The ranger-type unit marched through extremely dense jungles, scaled jagged mountains, crossed swiftly flowing rivers, and battled with exotic animals to join forces with the surviving Merrill's Marauders in Burma. The group of young soldiers became known as the "Mars Task Force."

Did you do all that, Daddy? Did you hike through jungles filled with swarms of black flies and bushes heavily laden with blood-sucking leeches?

I wrote a letter to the Veterans Administration in Montgomery, Alabama, requesting your medical records. I persuaded Momma to sign the release form, and months later an oversized manila envelope arrived in the mail. Inside were copies of your physical induction into the army, March 1944, at Fort McPherson, Georgia. You weighed only 120 pounds when you were nineteen years old and signed the document that changed your life forever.

I sat for days trying to decipher the hastily scribbled words on the bulk of the papers written by field doctors and surgeons describing the traumatic wounds you received to your hand at a place called Tonkwa in north Burma on December 15, 1944.

"On that day, casualties were light, but at 1200 hours, Private Dalton F. Williams was struck by a .25 caliber Japanese bullet during the final hours of enemy action. The bullet entered his left hand at the index finger, traumatically amputating it, and then

traversed through the 3rd and 4th fingers, where it exited, taking the pinkie with it."

The report states they performed two surgeries at the 20th General Hospital in India to try to repair the damage to your hand. I cried when I read the part where one doctor suggested amputating your whole hand. He wrote in his report, "The patient adamantly refused." It's no wonder you always disliked hospitals and doctors.

Every night, I'm sure you relived the weary hours of moving through the Burmese jungles, because I vividly remember you suffering from horrible nightmares. Those midnight hours you awoke drenched in sweat were probably from fighting to escape the stinging insects, poisonous snakes, chattering baboons, and unbearable heat.

I wish you could have told me some of the things I found out about you over the past few years, but I realize now that it was too painful for you to speak of the harrowing experiences you lived through as a young man. You were probably just trying to protect me and spare me from the violent details.

Daddy, I finally understand why you were always so quiet and could sit alone for hours at a time. I'm sorry for getting mad at your silence, and I hope you know that even when I was upset with you, I still loved you very much.

Momma and I went to the government building in Gadsden, Alabama, where Congressman Aderholt issued us the nine medals you earned in World War II but never received. The Purple Heart and the Bronze Star have your name engraved on the back. They are so beautiful. I wish you could see them.

Please, don't be angry with me for digging up all this about your past. While writing your obituary for the newspaper, the man at the funeral home wanted to know where you fought in the war and which medals you had received. I cried because I couldn't answer his questions. I wasn't ready to let go of you when cancer stole you away from me forever.

Finding that box in the attic kept you with me a little while longer and gave me a reason to climb out of bed each day. It has been five years and I still miss you so much.

All of my life, you were my hero, and now that you are recognized as an American hero as well, I have never been more proud to be your daughter.

Rest in peace, Daddy. I love you.

Your baby girl,
Sandy ∽

When Pop-Pop Was a Pillar

by Marcia E. Brown | *Muskogee, Oklahoma*

WHEN I RECENTLY DROVE into Muskogee, Oklahoma, where I spent most of my childhood, I felt sure that I could find my way around. But within minutes I was lost. Too many landmarks had disappeared.

After wandering in our old neighborhood where the proud Victorian houses of my grandparents' block once stood, I finally found a familiar sight: the First Baptist Church.

I parked in front and memories of attending this church with my grandfather, whom I called Pop-Pop, flooded back.

I remembered skipping along the sidewalk, my small hand tucked warmly in Pop-Pop's large hand. Taking care not to scuff my good shoes, I skipped in joy and also because it was my way of keeping up with Pop-Pop's long strides.

I was five years old, thin and small for my age. Pop-Pop was sixty-one and six feet tall. On that autumn morning, the eastern Oklahoma air was crisp and clear and Pop-Pop and I were on our way to Sunday school. Back at the sprawling frame house that sheltered three generations of our family during the Great Depression years, Grandma and my mother were nursing colds.

◄○►

During my childhood days in the 1930s, when Mama and I, and sometimes Dad and my uncle, lived with Mom's parents, Pop-Pop and I had a Sunday routine. I treasured those times.

Most mornings, Pop-Pop and I rose earlier than everyone else. I was attuned to listen for his steps and the way he cleared his throat as he passed my bedroom door. Even before the aroma of percolating coffee drifted upstairs, I was out of bed, hurrying to dress and join him in the kitchen. On chilly mornings, by the time I got downstairs, Pop-Pop would have already stoked the coal furnace to warm the house.

On Sundays, I knew that by the time I washed and put on my best dress and shoes, Pop-Pop would have a special breakfast prepared for us. Scrambled eggs, bacon, and toast slathered liberally with homemade grape jelly would be waiting on the kitchen table. After breakfast, if weather permitted, we walked to the drugstore to buy Sunday newspapers: *The Tulsa World, The Daily Oklahoman*, and, on special occasions, *The Kansas City Star*. Three sets of comics were an unusual treat that Pop-Pop reserved for after Sunday dinner when I'd sit on his lap and he'd read the comics aloud to me.

Back home, Pop-Pop slung the papers onto the library table that stood between his favorite chair and Grandma's.

"Sunday school time!" he called. "Do you know your Bible verse?"

"Yes!" I answered and recited it. It was Pop-Pop who most often helped me learn the required weekly verse.

As always, Pop-Pop walked me right to the classroom door, making sure I had a nickel contribution tied in a corner of the handkerchief in my pocket before he left.

The church seemed enormous to me, and the crowds of people overwhelming. Pop-Pop understood this and never failed to be at the door to pick me up when the class ended. Together we walked to the sanctuary, stopping often while he spoke with friends. At last we were seated in our usual pew near the back.

Pop-Pop's singing voice was loud and clear. He was partial to the older hymns he had learned as a boy. I loved the music, especially when the organ was loud. Before I was old enough to read the words and music, Pop-Pop sometimes let me stand on the pew leaning against him, watching as his finger traced the lines in the hymnal. He did the same with his well-worn Bible. I quietly watched his finger follow verses read aloud in the service. As a small child, I did not understand the sermon, which seemed to last a *very long time,* but when I was with Pop-Pop, I did not mind. Pop-Pop had a constant cough, and always carried Life Savers with him. At the beginning of the sermon, he quietly extracted one peppermint Life Saver for each of us. Then he whispered, "See if you can make it last through the whole sermon. Don't chomp it."

Concentrating on that kept me occupied.

Leaving church seemed to take as long as the sermon had, for everybody wanted to have a word with Pop-Pop. He seemed to know everyone! Many members were also his patients, for he had been one of the first two dentists to set up practice when Muskogee was still in Indian Territory.

On that particular fall Sunday, as we descended the wide front steps of the church, someone patted me on the head and said, "Aren't you proud of your grandfather! He's a pillar of the church." At age five, that was a puzzling and worrisome remark to me.

"What's a pillar?" I asked Mama later.

"It's like one of those tall columns across the front of the church," she said, without a clue as to my question's context. "Pillars inside the building hold up the roof."

I did not understand. If Pop-Pop was a pillar of the church, what held it up when he was not there? Or would he turn into one of those white columns across the front of the building? Had they all been grandpas at one time? Is that what happened to grandfathers when they grew old?

I became terrified that Pop-Pop might suddenly turn into a tall, silent column.

"Don't die, Pop-Pop!" I pleaded as I climbed onto his lap that afternoon when he was ready to read our favorite comic strips aloud. "Please don't be a pillar!"

It took some time and a lot of explaining before he understood my fears. Then he laughed and laughed, hugging me so I knew everything was all right.

"Don't worry, little one," he reassured me. "I'll always be just Pop-Pop."

Sixty-five years have passed since that Sunday. But you just never know, so today, before driving on, I smiled as I blew a kiss toward the church pillars. ∽

The Penny Block

by Lad Moore | *Parrott, Georgia*

AFTER YEARS OF OILING, the heart-pine floors in the Penny Moore Grocery gleamed like marble. Each Saturday after closing, my grandfather flooded the floor with a reddish liquid, and mopped it vigorously into the wood, allowing that Sunday would give the floor ample drying time. The oil smelled of cinnamon, but he warned me that it was not.

In contrast to the slick pine of the grocery area, the meat market floor was covered with sawdust, with a glass meat counter as its centerpiece. Within it, slabs of beef, bacon, and pork lay facing the rows of fryers like opposing armies—separated only by a line of parsley and sliced lemons. To the rear of the counter lay the more unheralded of nature's bounty. Calves' tongues, pigs' feet, and jars of chitterlings made up a circus sideshow of culinary oddities. Nestled among them, in trays of chipped ice, were jars of brains, surrounded by chicken eggs in a pinwheel design.

Grandpa explained that the arrangement was not just artistry—it was the custom to cook scrambled eggs with fresh brains.

I loved eggs, and to me it seemed a disgrace to ask eggs to humiliate themselves that way.

The hallmark of the butcher shop was its chopping block. Its surface was scooped out from assaults by long knives and harsh scrapings, endured throughout its lifetime. Its columnar legs were reminiscent of the entrances to grand hotels. I crawled under the block's canopy many times, watching my grandfather's boots move about. Stenciled underneath the block was the name MICHIGAN MAPLE BLOCK, SAGINAW. I could reach the words with an extended arm, and I memorized them by tracing the letters with my finger. My imagination soon took me to that place called Saginaw. I could see men sawing and finishing Grandpa's block, then lifting it into a truck for the long trip to Texas. It took four stout men to load it, one man to lovingly cover it with canvas and tie it so that it would not tip.

From underneath the block, I sometimes had to dodge the crimson raindrops of freshly butchered hogs as the drips speckled the sawdust beside me. The cutting was swift, and soon the hog's stripped bones filled the bone box across the room. Twice a week a man came by to empty the box. "Bound for the meal plant," he once explained. I wondered … what kind of meal? Not oatmeal, not cornmeal? The more I thought about it, the more I began to suspect grits. "Grit," after all, sounded deceptive enough to be a code word for ground-up bones. I had long wondered why grits came to my plate always disguised with a coverlet of butter or gravy.

The Penny Moore Grocery on Garrett Street stood for thirty years. After the end of World War II, its almost rural setting was engulfed within a housing project known as "Yankee Stadium"—so named for the circular pattern of jammed-together houses that ringed the hillsides. The store eventually failed, as did Grandpa two years later. I was told that its demise was due to bad debt—excess credit extended to the returning soldiers without jobs who moved into the Stadium. It was sad to see the abandoned store pass into decay, and after high school I was relieved to leave Garrett Street far behind. I graduated from college and immersed myself in the corporate world.

At the behest of my company, I relocated nine times during my career. One duty station was in Georgia, during the Carter presidential campaign. My wife, Kay, and I often visited his hometown, in Plains, in a futile effort to see the president-to-be. Instead, we had to settle for some of the other, more colorful family members. Brother Billy was usually available to autograph beer cans, and Miss Lillian, the matriarch, was frequently seen buzzing with reporters.

The road to Plains passed through the nearly abandoned town of Parrott. On one of our trips, we noticed that the old general store was open, having always been closed before. We wandered in and were greeted by an old gentleman who invited us to browse around. The store was like a museum, having been shuttered since its heyday thirty years before. I discovered a rack of Luden's cough drops, the packages still tightly wrapped in original cellophane, still marked ten cents.

In the back of the store was a meat market, and behind the counter sat a butcher block piled high with wet, rotting newspapers. For the first time in years, my mind raced back to the days of Penny Moore. The block was similar to Grandpa's but more rectangular. I removed the newspapers layer by layer, exposing rat droppings. Imagine my disappointment when I removed the last layer and revealed a deeply rotted, spongy gray surface. I was about to walk away when I noticed the knife rack attached to the end. Stenciled on it were the words MICHIGAN MAPLE BLOCK.

My hand rushed to my mouth to cover the gushing excitement. I had to have this old block! The storeowner was hesitant, muttering something about mounting a vise on it for his workshop. I convinced him the surface of the block was far too decayed for that. We struck a bargain, and I returned two days later with a truck and some friends to load it.

Using a crosscut saw, Kay and I removed layers of the block surface until we found fresh maple. After days of sanding and smoothing, we finished it with several coats of polyurethane, each hand rubbed. It glistened like glass.

Now my block serves as an island in our kitchen, but it's not functional workspace—we dare not put a blade to it. Instead, it has become the window to my past. Today the Penny Moore Grocery lot stands empty. The building is gone, and only a ribbon of concrete that was once its sidewalk remains. At the walk's end, an oak tree has pushed the concrete into a tentlike position, testimony to the tree's will over man's. Like the sidewalk, my childhood memories had been shoved aside by the march of years and my focus elsewhere. The block brought them back.

On one of her visits and without any prompting from me, my granddaughter discovered the secret refuge between its columnar legs. As she peeked up at me, I saw myself in her face—her freckles reminding me of crumbs of sawdust from Penny Moore's. ∿

The House in the Picture

by Kelly L. Stone | *Flowery Branch, Georgia*

MY FATHER EASES himself from the car, astonishment on his face.

"The house where I was born and raised is only fifteen minutes from here!" he exclaims. My mouth drops open.

"You mean the house in the picture?"

In my living room, I have an old photo of the home belonging to my great-grandfather, where my father was born in 1932. In the picture, my great-grandparents stare sternly at the camera, their hard lives etched on their faces. The house they built by hand looms up behind them.

"The very same," Dad says, pleased.

We get back in the car and I follow his directions north, leaving Atlanta behind. Fifteen minutes later, we see the hand-painted sign that has directed travelers to Oakwood, Georgia, for five decades. The road takes us beside the old train station, now a post office. I look at my father, whose face has gone soft with melancholy.

We follow Allen Road into Oakwood. The town has changed little in the forty years since my father left. He points out landmarks as we pass them—the red brick Baptist church with the black bell hanging in its little tower, the train tracks that wink at us through the thick pine trees and that run only a quarter of a mile from his childhood home. I remember hearing the train's sweet whistles as I slept in the handmade featherbed I shared with my grandmother. Around the corner is a cemetery that seemed huge when I was a child, but now seems tiny in comparison to most.

"Remember when we used to walk through there?" Dad asks.

"Yes," I reply. "We tried to see who could find the oldest birth dates."

Allen Road winds through the residential part of town. Every house has a wide front porch, screen doors to let the magnolia-scented air in, and swings that hang from giant silver hooks screwed into the ceiling. We follow the railroad tracks to the city of Flowery Branch, passing a tiny white church that is dwarfed by an oak tree.

"My grandfather walked to that church every Sunday morning," Dad says. "No matter what the weather, no matter how much whiskey he'd put down the night before."

Above the church is another cemetery. My father's grandparents and great-grandparents are buried there. Most of the headstones are so old the names are wearing off. We stop and walk around, brushing leaves off of the graves. Some of the birthdates go back to the mid-1800s. Dad stands in front of his grandfather's grave, lips twitching.

Later, we drive toward a dirt road named Ed Cobb Road. Ed Cobb was my father's grandfather.

"Here it is," Dad says as a large meadow opens before us. "And there's my home." My eyes follow his to a two-story wooden structure, the house in the picture. A garage has been added, and a wheelchair ramp for the current occupant, but other than that, time hasn't touched the house. The cement stairs in front sag heavily into the ground. The windows, warped with age, reflect the low gray clouds in the sky. We get out and walk to the door. Dad knocks. An elderly woman peers out through the window.

"I was born here," Dad says loudly because the woman won't open the door. "My grandfather was Ed Cobb." The woman's face brightens and she smiles, but still she won't open the door.

"Mind if we walk around?" I holler. The woman shakes her head.

Dad and I stand for a while under the canopy of trees that arch over Ed Cobb Road, the street built and named by my great-grandfather. The property was sold off over the years as the family struggled to survive, and now individual houses dot the landscape that once had been dense woods.

"The barn is still there," Dad says, nodding his head in the direction of a rust-colored structure.

"I wonder if the wringer-style washing machine is still in there," I say, thinking of the first time I helped my grandmother wash clothes. I had stared in amazement at the open-topped machine that swished the dirty clothes back and forth in the gray water, while she cautioned me to keep my fingers out of the way as we fed the wet clothes through the wringer on top, the water squirting out, splashing my shoes.

"And there's the well we drank from," Dad says, looking at a lopsided stack of red bricks. "That water tasted better than any I've ever had."

Down a steep slope, Dad shows me the creek that he used to bathe in because the house had no running water. He tells me about how he and his buddies used to go drag-racing on the few area roads that were paved in the 1950s. He worked in a grocery store down the street, which is long gone. He takes several deep breaths, trying to summon the scent of his youth. I peer through the trees to the house behind us, reconciling the renovated structure with the house in the picture on my wall back home. My father is a million miles away, back in his youth, back in the time when life was long and fully ahead of him.

When he is ready to leave, I drive slowly beside the railroad tracks toward the interstate. Dad turns in the seat and watches the town of his youth recede behind us.

"Hasn't changed much, has it?" he says, mostly to himself.

"The house looks just like it does in the picture," I agree.

Dad wipes a rugged hand across his face to keep me from seeing the tears that slip down his cheeks. Then he nods solemnly. "It was good to go home." ∾

Home Away from Home

by Beverly Carol Lucey | *Peabody, Massachusetts*

MOVING FROM A SMALL NEW ENGLAND TOWN to Atlanta, Georgia, created more than a bit of culture shock in my life. Since birth, I'd hugged the coastline, and now I was living inland. My past, my friends, and my family were now thousands of miles away. I was staying afloat on a wavy memory until my new friend, Julie, suggested we head for a huge flea market called Lakewood. Lakewood, it seemed, would have to do when the ocean was not handy, and despite what I might have thought I'd find in Lakewood, I hadn't expected a miracle. But that's exactly what happened.

Past the booth with bright ceramic tiles, and the one with World War II artifacts, to the left of bobbing bird lawn ornaments, I spied two things I would have sworn came straight from my parents' South Peabody basement. One was a rusted TV tray, with a painted cabbage rose and plastic clips that allowed it to fold and fit into the trunk of my dad's salmon-and-gray '55 Chevy. The other was the exact red-and-gray heavy metal jug we used to fill with cold drink concoctions and bring to the beach. I was transported.

To make the trek to the beach, my family needed time, thought, and a list. It wasn't easy.

Young men in 1950s movies swept into parking lots in old Chevy convertibles, hopped out with towels, and then ran like wild colts into the sea. They didn't bring food, lunch money, or a blanket. With names like Todd, Tab, and Troy, they easily found a blanket on the beach with the prettiest girls, girls with flat stomachs, girls with sandwiches, who'd rub their backs with Sea & Ski. Transistor radios rocked. Volleyball or games of catch allowed Todd, Tab, and Troy to strut their bare-skinned stuff.

The rest of us—back in the real world—were with our families. Basically, we moved everything portable into the car, updated with this year's beach sticker, and headed out around four in the afternoon. We had only the one car, so we couldn't go earlier. Not on a weekday. My father had to finish his factory shift, sweating in the impossible heat on iron floors, while two of my friends and I languished, twelve-year-old misfits, on my front porch, gasping for air. We were bored, inert, suspended in the heat.

When my father came home in our nonconvertible Chevy, we started loading: heavy, aluminum, full-length, webbed folding chairs; big, frayed towels used only for the beach; a wicker basket with fried chicken, cookies, washed grapes, peaches, and watermelon slices in aluminum foil; the hibachi for those nights it would be too hot to sleep inland and we planned to stay past eight. And, of course, the bag of charcoal.

Packed around us in the back seat was a heavy gray metal drink container with a leaky spigot. Somewhere in the back seat, in a paper bag, bright, iridescent aluminum tumblers in different colors rattled. Another heavy metal cooler held potato salad, coleslaw, and tuna salad packed in ice. Every mother we knew feared poisoning her family with mayonnaise products gone bad. A leather-encased radio with huge batteries would keep us up with the Red Sox.

Another crinkly grocery bag held changes of clothes—God forbid we should get chilled or chaffed.

Water has a perfect memory, according to writer Toni Morrison, but our car was a desperate attempt not to forget something, anything, that could be needed. Our slow departure from the front of the house was punctuated by my mother's panic about forgetting.

"Oh! The mustard! Wait! Let me see if I packed Band-Aids. Matches! Frank? You got matches?"

My father would slam on the brakes at each outburst until we turned the corner. I'd smile in the back seat as soon as we sped around the corner, knowing there was no turning back now. "Too late, Ma," I'd whisper.

We lit punks against mosquitoes, used washcloths for sticky hands, lugged metal TV trays to keep the ants off of the food. We brought everything that did not need a plug, dragging it all toward my parents' friends from the old neighborhood who set up housekeeping on the hilly part of the seaside park where the best breeze was. The others brought enough for lunch and supper. Most weren't cooks. They didn't make the effort the way my mother did. They'd tossed together salami, pickles, big bags of chips, maybe bottles of Moxie, Nehi, and Squirt, ice cubes melting around them.

Up there, with the occasional breeze ruffling our hair and making us dive for flying napkins, we created a small, temporary town where everyone knew everyone. We were all safe, even from the heat.

In my mind, the memory grows slowly dark as dusk descends and the tide of thoughts moves closer. My mother and her friend Irene talk softly. One of them barks out a bawdy laugh, but by now I can't see who. Maybe my father is smoking a cigarette, or has fallen asleep and missed Ted Williams's home run. Maybe Jane, Arlene, and I are deciding that while Pat Boone is probably a nice guy, it doesn't mean that Elvis is the opposite. Even with those hips.

Maybe I'm full of hamburgers; maybe I'm finally feeling cooled off. Maybe the night sounds at Lynch Park Beach were the cradle of my childhood where we carried our home whenever we went and it was heavy, and solid, and very, very good. Maybe, unlike the water, my memory is not perfect. But, then again, maybe it is.

I went home from Lakeview with the TV tray and the heavy metal jug stuffed in the back seat, rattling against one another in a memory that will forever be mine. ∾

A Precious Memory

by Grace Walker Looper | *Glen Alpine, North Carolina*

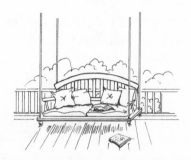

I FOUND IT WHILE SPRING-CLEANING. It was only a tiny clothespin, but it brought with it a flood of memories. As I gripped the small object tightly in my hand, I felt the years melt away.

It was a tough time for families everywhere. In an attempt to bring the country out of the Depression, President Franklin Roosevelt had just established the New Deal. My father worked for the Public Works Administration and helped build roads and dams, and also worked on other federal projects. Families in Glen Alpine, North Carolina, had little money to spend on nonessentials, but my four-year-old mind knew only that my daddy went off to work every day.

As I held the tiny clothespin in my hand, I remembered sitting on the floor, my eyes glued on an advertisement I'd found in a catalog. It featured a wondrous "drink and wet" baby doll with marvelous accessories—a bottle, clothing, diapers, a wash tub, a clothesline, and, of course, the clothespins—all packed in a carrying case. I had pored over the picture for days and knew every item by heart.

The next morning, as Daddy got ready for work, I ran up to him, bubbling over with excitement. "Daddy, see this doll?" I asked, pointing to the picture. He knelt down beside me and looked as I listed all the items that came with the doll.

"Isn't it the bestest, Daddy? Please get it for me and don't forget the clothespins. They're so little and cute."

My father, a man of few words, hugged me and said, "We'll see."

All day my excitement mounted. I could hardly wait until he came home with my doll.

My mother tried to prepare me for disappointment, but I wouldn't listen to reason.

"Daddy will do it," I declared. I knew Daddy would bring me the doll.

"Grace, you must remember that Daddy doesn't have much money and the doll costs a lot," Mama said, trying a different approach. But nothing my mother said dampened my enthusiasm.

Long before it was time for Daddy to arrive home from work, I positioned myself at the window to wait. Finally, I saw him walking down the road. I jumped up and dashed out the door.

"Grace, honey, come back," my mother called.

Ignoring her, I ran on to meet my daddy and get my new doll. As I got closer to him, I saw he was carrying his black metal lunchbox in one hand and what looked like a suitcase in the other.

"My doll!" I cried as I reached for him. "My doll! I knew you would get my doll, Daddy." He switched his lunchbox to the hand with the case and hoisted me up.

"I couldn't disappoint my little girl," he said.

Now, as I stand holding the clothespin, I realize that he had never disappointed me. He'd always been there to get me all the things I needed and some of the things I didn't need but desperately wanted. Buying that doll meant he wasn't able to purchase something *he* might have needed. Through the years, my daddy was always there for me, offering me security and love no matter what form of sacrifice it meant for him. ∿

Crossing Bridges

by Penny Porter | *Esopus, New York*

I KNOW A TINY TOWN NAMED ESOPUS. An Indian legend tells us Esopus means "water running backward." Indeed, the creek that connects the village to New York State's mighty Hudson flows away from the river, instead of emptying into it.

Esopus is simply one more little town that has managed to forever stand still in America. With few changes, its heart still beats from the corner grocery store, now a motorcycle repair shop, and the nearby post office window, gas pump, and firehouse. Up the street, the three-room rural grade school still faces Highway 9W. Voices of children continue to echo.

Esopus may have been a whistle-stop town in the late 1930s, when I was a child, but to think it hasn't changed since the late 1800s makes this girl sit up and take notice.

My great-grandfather, Alton Brooks Parker, former chief judge of the New York Court of Appeals, lived in this small hamlet. In 1904, Esopus became a hub of activity when he ran against Theodore Roosevelt for president. Soundly defeated, Judge Parker smiled his relief, returned to his bench in New York City on weekdays,

◄○►

and traveled by train on weekends to farm his beloved Esopus land. Famous for a few months, the little town settled back into its quiet history to rest.

The judge's home and land remained in our family, and, as a child, I occasionally visited my aunt who lived there for more than sixty years. Sitting on the lawn in front of the house overlooking the Hudson, I lived in a world of dreams—that world where a lonely child becomes a creator. I especially loved imagining about the people who lived in a house across the river, in a town called Hyde Park. Perhaps they had children? Their name was Roosevelt. In my dreams, I built bridges across the Hudson, so I could go over and play. But would they play with a child so tall and sickly, so different that others teased and made fun of her?

One afternoon when I was in my early teens, my aunt and I took the train from Esopus to New York City. She planned a trip to Best and Company's lingerie department on Fifth Avenue to buy some new "brassieres," a word a young girl would be too embarrassed to utter in those days. While all seventy-nine pounds of my 6'1" frame cowered round-shouldered and miserable beside a rack of satin and rubber girdles, a lady as tall as me appeared. In moments, she and my aunt were giggling and laughing between privacy curtains in the far corner. I overheard details about bones, stays, hooks, and eyes rubbing a blister right in the middle of the back; double Ds (whatever they were); and the benefits of the delightful invention of lamb's wool cushions to prevent shoulder grooves.

Every so often the lady peeked out at me and smiled. I felt heat rush to my face. She was over six feet tall, a monstrous height at that time for a woman. Yet, she walked with dignity and grace.

Finally, after my aunt and her newfound friend had made their purchases and promised to get together soon for tea at The Plaza, they both came over to me, now more hunched and unsure than ever, huddling near the elevator.

"This is my niece, Penny," said Aunt Mary.

"I'm happy to meet you," I stammered, offering my hand. The lady didn't reply. Instead, she looked me straight in the eye, took my hand in hers, and with the index finger on her other hand, stabbed me gently but repeatedly in the middle of my bony chest.

"Stand tall and straight, dear child," she said, "or one day those ribs are going to poke a hole straight through your heart."

A thousand needles pricked my scalp. Blood scorched my cheeks. Her words hurt, but I listened. I learned. And I understood. I put my shoulders back, took a deep breath, and began to hold my head up high.

Years later, after I became a writer, I went back to visit Esopus with my husband and six children. During a quiet moment alone, I stood once again on the East bank of the Hudson, recalling the bridges I'd built to the other side. But it was that bridge in my teens, that unforgettable connection that gave me the courage to face the world, for which I will be forever grateful. The memory of that one-day trip to the lingerie department of Best and Company in New York City, where the words and wisdom of the first lady of the United States of America changed the life of a lonely young girl, will remain with me forever.

"Stand tall and straight, dear child," said Eleanor Roosevelt, "or one day those ribs are going to poke a hole straight through your heart." ∾

Esopus, New York

Population: 9,331

Town Facts

First incorporated • Esopus was officially incorporated in 1811. However, the tiny hamlet of Esopus voted to be left out of the incorporation with a neighboring hamlet called Port Ewen. The little village, to this day, is simply a postal stop and firehouse, and boasts approximately 100 residents.

Transportation • Ulster County Rural Transportation, a bus service.

Location • The town of Esopus is located in Ulster County, on the west bank of the majestic Hudson River, nearly 100 miles north of New York City. To the north is Rondout Creek; to the south is Highland, in the town of Lloyd; and to the west are the towns of Rosendale and New Paltz. The town covers about forty square miles, much of which is woodlands filled with natural beauty. Rivers in the area include the Hudson, Walkill, Rondout Creek, Black Creek, and Swartekil Creek.

Places of note • Several communities make up the town of Esopus, including Connelly, Esopus, New Salem, Port Ewen, Rifton, St. Remy, Sleightsburgh, Ulster Park, Union Center, and West Park. A Dutch Reformed church built in 1827 is now home to the Klyne Esopus Museum.

It's All in a Name

*I*n the early 1600s, land to the west side of the Hudson River and south of the Rondout Creek was known by the English and Dutch as a good place to trade with the Native Americans from the Algonquian Nation, who called the area *esepu,* or "rivulet," depending who you ask. The town's name can also be traced back to several additional meanings, including "high banks" or "water running backward." The town that sprang up in the area was fittingly named Esopu, in honor of its early people.

The name Esopus was first recorded on a map in 1616, as the name of the village on the east shore of the Hudson River, in present-day Dutchess County. It is assumed the name was transferred to the west side, at the mouth of the Rondout Creek, by early 1620. ∾

People from the Past

*J*ohn Burroughs, an Esopus resident from 1873 until his death in 1921, was a prolific writer. He was so enamored of nature that he built a rustic log cabin in the backwoods and from there authored some twenty-five books about nature. It was from this very spot that he entertained Thomas Edison, Henry Ford, and John Muir, who respected his life's work. Following his death, the John Burroughs Association was formed. The Association's goal is to preserve places associated with Burroughs's life.

Alton Brooks Parker, also known as Alton B. Parker, former chief judge of the New York Court of Appeals, was a candidate in the 1904 presidential election.

Sojourner Truth, a freed slave and an abolitionist and past resident of Esopus, stood six feet tall and stood up for the rights of black women. She is remembered for a particular speech, given during a women's rights conference, in which she bared her breast to prove she was, in fact, a woman, different from a white woman only in the color of her skin and the fact that she did not receive the same rights. ∾

Skipping Stones

by Merry Simmons | *Ringsted, Iowa*

My father was an Air Force officer. We moved a lot. But wherever Dad was stationed, we always made the twice-yearly trek to see my grandparents in Ringsted, Iowa. We would come for Christmas, battling our way over icy roads, the tire chains sending strange vibrations through the car. We also came in the summer, heat-hazed fields of corn flashing by the open car windows, sweaty legs sticking to the seats.

Ringsted was a little piece of Denmark that had taken root in the rich black soil of northern Iowa. It was a place where everyone was named Petersen or Christiansen or Johansen or Andreasen; where all were related in some sort of shirttail way, the labyrinth of kinship both confusing and comforting. These people would float through my grandparents' home in ever-changing patterns, consuming vast quantities of strong black coffee and dainty open-faced sandwiches, occasionally lapsing into a language I didn't understand but whose cadence still whispers in my blood.

Such conversation was eventually boring to a six-year-old, however, so after I'd made my requisite appearance and spoken politely to all assembled, I was freed to roam the confines of the house. Like most dwellings of its time, my grandparents' home had odd cubbyholes filled with the debris of living, irresistible treasure troves for an inquisitive child. It was in one such place that I found the Roy Tan cigar box in the middle of a precariously balanced stack of books. The box was heavy; it rattled. I eagerly flipped back the lid, expecting to find something wonderful. To my disappointment, the box contained only rocks—mud colored, flat, and smooth. But someone had thought to save them, so I sought some explanation of their value.

I found my grandfather in the glider on the front porch, smoking one of those smelly cigars that Grandma didn't allow in the house.

"Whatcha got there, Pumpkin?" he asked.

"Rocks," I answered, opening the box for his inspection.

He picked one up, fitting it deftly between his thumb and index finger. He smiled. "Skipping stones," he said. "They must have been your father's. As a boy he was very good at skipping stones."

Now, I could skip, but I didn't know what stones had to do with the activity. When I said this to Grandpa, he launched into a tale of my dad's skill at bouncing stones across a pond's surface. With every word, my wonder grew. My father? Had the stern disciplinarian I knew ever been a laughing boy throwing stones?

When I said as much to Grandpa, he picked up another stone and told me of a boy who'd painted the eggs in Mrs. Johansen's henhouse and then put them back under the chickens. With another stone he told me of Reverend Lund's wagon magically appearing on top of a grain elevator.

"It took your father and three friends all night to take the wagon apart and reassemble it again." Grandpa chuckled. "I tanned him good, but mostly for climbing up so high. The very idea scared your grandma to death."

Sitting there on the glider, in the midst of a cloud of redolent smoke, Grandpa created a person I'd never known. I had trouble getting my mind around the idea of my father as a mischievous boy. The revelations were amazing.

"We'll go over to Torklesen's pond tomorrow and I'll show you how these work," he said, ruffling my hair, and then he returned to coffee and sandwiches and talk.

Grandpa was a man of his word. The next day, we hiked to the edge of town, where a small pond caught the blue sky and held it suspended in a brilliant green field. I carried the skipping stones, but when we got to the water, I couldn't bring myself to throw any of them. Each seemed an entry into a part of my father's life that I found fascinating. In the end, Grandpa and I each found our own stones, maybe not as flat or thin as the ones in the box, but decidedly ours.

We threw stones until my arm was sore. I managed to get some to skip three times, which Grandpa convinced me was a real accomplishment. In memory, I can still feel the tingle of pride mixed with the warmth of the sun on my legs.

Time has turned the pages of my book. Some chapters have finished and new ones have begun. But I still have the cigar box of skipping stones. The box is more battered. The once-proud red banner that proclaims THE CIGARS THAT BREATHE is now murky pink. The stones are as they have always been, however—flat and smooth, shaped for a child's hand. I used them to introduce my son to pieces of his grandfather that weren't readily apparent. I keep them so my grandsons may know a man they will never meet.

But under my watch, none of the stones will ever be used. I've come to discover that when each of us faces the rippling surface of life, it's better if we choose our own skipping stones, which will then either sink or skip from the power of our own personal throw. ∾

Home Delivery

by Genevieve Williams | *Trenton, New Jersey*

Do you believe that dealers are now getting two dollars apiece for old glass milk bottles? I made this discovery while strolling through one of those new co-op junk/antique shops. Those places always evoke memories of times gone by, but the milk bottles took me way back.

Life on the Delaware River in the late 1930s and early '40s was tough, but we did have one luxury: home delivery. Not only the daily newspapers but also groceries, milk, eggs, and even dry cleaning were delivered. We lived just south of Trenton, New Jersey, in a houseboat docked at my father's boatyard. We had no car and had to walk at least a half mile to the bus. Home delivery was a real boon.

Each morning, Mother called in her grocery order and it would be delivered that afternoon. Of course, it made it easy that there were a limited number of options for each item. You could order a tube of toothpaste and not have to indicate whether you wanted "extra whitening power," "tartar control," "mint-flavored," or any of the other varieties available today. Toothpaste was toothpaste and that was it. Mother also trusted the grocer to "pick out a nice plump chicken" and he trusted us to pay our bill at the end of the month. The question of paper or plastic was never an issue. The groceries were delivered in boxes.

Deliveries by the Egg Lady were always interesting to me. She usually had time to come in for a cup of tea and a chat with my mother. Her Nordic fairness was an anomaly in our Italian-American neighborhood. The blue veins I could see through her nearly transparent white skin fascinated me. I expected her to keel over at any moment, believing that her pallor meant she was sick. Mother used the opportunity to explain that white eggs and brown eggs were equally good; they just looked different.

My favorite treat had to do with the milk delivery. Back then, milk was delivered in one-quart glass bottles with little round cardboard caps. It also was not homogenized, which meant that the cream rose to the top. The milk was delivered very early in the morning and left in a lead-lined wooden box on the dock. Sometimes in the winter it was so cold out there that the milk froze and the expanding cream popped the cap off of the bottle. Mother would scoop a big spoonful of this frozen cream into a dish and pour a little Hershey's syrup over the top for me. What a treat, an ice-cream sundae for breakfast!

As I grow older and driving becomes a chore, I think longingly of the days of home delivery. How wonderful it would be to have fresh milk delivered to my door twice a week. And a cup of tea and a chat with the Egg Lady would make my day. ᜮ

Starting Life at the Top

Jimmy George as told to Nan B. Clark | *Beverly, Massachusetts*

THEY WERE BOTH nineteen years old in 1908. Stella, my mother, was a maid up at the big house and Jimmy, my father, was a groom. He lived above the stable all year round, and this was where they honeymooned, and then where I came into the world.

Mr. and Mrs. Robert Evans owned Dawson Hall. In those days, Beverly, Massachusetts, was part of what the newspapers called "The Gold Coast," which meant that quite a few wealthy people built big places right on the ocean north of Boston, but didn't use them much. They left a handful of natives like my parents to keep things going.

How did my folks ever stay warm that winter?

That's what I always asked them, living as they did high above the stables in the attic of the huge carriage barn. Dad would shrug and say "Love," but I think it was probably the cookstove. Even today, you can see the stovepipe jutting up through the broken shingles, making a fine perch for the gulls.

"Can you hold on, sweetheart?" my father asked my mother over and over again on the night I was about to come into the world. "Can you hold on until the doctor gets here?"

◄○►

According to my mother, she laughed, squeezed his hand, and replied, "Doctor? Jimmy, no doctor's going to come out here in a blizzard. Face it, darling, we're on our own."

They took some comfort in the knowledge that the housekeeper and a skeleton staff were still in residence in Dawson Hall, the three-story mansion out on the very tip of the point jutting into Beverly Harbor. That was where my dad had gone to use the hand-cranked telephone, leaving a message with the doctor's wife.

Much to their surprise, they heard a muffled pounding at the huge double doors just as Mother reached what she called "the interesting part." When Dad was finally able to wrench one of the doors open, panting from his race down the narrow back stairs, the doctor blew in on a cloud of swirling snow.

I sometimes even think I remember it all, the way the kerosene lamp glowed on the loving faces hovering around me, the pungent odor of wood crackling in that little cast-iron stove, the restless nickering of the horses down below, and above all, the rise and fall of the ocean smashing against the seawall at the base of the carriage barn.

In reality, I can't remember anything at all about living there, since we moved in the spring. Although I never told Dad, I've always felt that was kind of a shame, because President William Howard Taft rented another estate on the property the very next summer. But my dad had found a better-paying job at a local manufacturing company.

Strangely enough, the day before President Taft was due to arrive, Mr. Evans took a spill from his horse. At first it seemed like he wasn't injured at all, but a few days later, he died. Although she carried on as best she could, Mrs. Evans died a few years later. Dawson Hall fell to the wreckers' ball after World War II, and the estate became a public park. Even after all these years, you can still walk through the Italian garden.

My birthplace hasn't been used for horses for over seventy years, but the grooved stone floors still mark the sluicing channels for the runoff when Dad washed the horses and Mrs. Evans's fancy carriage. The grain chute from the second floor is still intact, as is the eight-sided skylight that brought sunshine to the hay bales. I think Mother must have used some of that hay to stuff up the bed I was born on, but she'd never admit to it.

Even today, abandoned and forlorn as it is, the carriage barn still has an air of strength and stability. Those round windows and the shabby spot where the clock used to be still give it an air of elegance, but, oh, how beautiful it must have been when the honey-colored shingles were intact and the white balustrade ran the length of the roof.

I've always felt that being born on the Evans estate, even in a carriage barn, conferred some kind of grace to me, as if I had been born to wealth myself instead of in an attic. I suppose I feel that way because, right from the start, my existence was seen as the most precious gift two young parents could share. ⟳

Honor Roll

by Robert N. Going | *Amsterdam, New York*

My ATTIC IS A WONDERFUL PLACE: open, spacious, twenty feet from floor to peak, full-size windows on the ends and three dormers for light. It is everything an attic should be, filled with treasures of past generations, the accumulated junk of twenty-three years of marriage, and the remains of six or seven estates that wandered our way.

As I reestablished my law practice, I had been spending a bit of time up there, searching out old files and forms and office supplies. When my client base had doubled to two, I felt the immediate need for a notebook to keep track of things. There, on a shelf, was an old bound business journal, which I quickly grabbed. The first seventy pages were missing and the rest seemed blank. Perfect.

I figured it had belonged to my father when he practiced law, forty years ago. It wasn't mine. I had never been so extravagant as to purchase anything in hardcover.

Then, as I flipped through it one day, I realized that it was not as blank as I had once thought. It was not my father's after all, but my grandmother's, dating back to when she led the American Legion Auxiliary in the late 1940s.

There were five pages of entries in the middle of the book, all in the neat handwriting of May Goodison Going Nichols, captioned "Deceased Amsterdam Boys of World War #2." I suspect she never finished the project, as the alphabetical listing ended abruptly with "Corp. Donald Suchiel, September 22, 1944, France." There were, nonetheless, 136 entries.

The magnitude of this small upstate New York mill town's loss stunned me. In ten years of Vietnam, there were less than a dozen deaths from this area.

Yet here were 136 names, from Private Leslie Ackerman to Corp. Donald Suchiel. The vast majority were in the years 1944 and 1945.

Aldi, Alibozek, Anderson. These fellows probably had adjoining lockers in high school.

William Hassenfuss, December 7, 1941, Hawaii. I ice-skated on the field named after him when I was a kid.

Norman Briskie, Eugene Greco, Allen Pileckas, Lawrence Quackenbush, Thomas Quigley, Thomas Rutkowski. Didn't I know all these guys? Well, I was born in 1951, so I couldn't have, but I suppose it should not be unusual that lads of my generation would bear the names of the honored dead.

Sgt. Sam Riccio, May 12, 1944, Germany. How often had I heard that name with affection over the years from his surviving kin? If he hadn't died in the war, I wonder if his niece would have been inspired to write that magnificent, powerful, awesome *Requiem* in the *Amsterdam Oratorio*.

Theodore Canape, Anthony DeStefano, Thomas DiCaprio, Mullarkey, Munroe, Murawski, Natoli.

There was a note next to Sgt. Richard Morties's name, which read, "Returned from overseas after having been a prisoner of war. Killed while on leave in auto accident in Fort Johnson, October 6, 1945."

Perkins, Petricca, Pettitti, Polikowski, Popielarz, Salvaleauskas, San Fillipo.

Sgt. Nicholas Foti, June 6, 1944, France; Private Harold Premo, June 6, 1944, Normandy; Pvt. John Schilling, June 6, 1944, France.

In another corner of the attic were letters my father had written to his mother during the war, including this one dated June 19, 1944, as he was about to sail for France and the fortnight-old Normandy campaign:

Dear Mom,

I'm sorry that I haven't written you sooner but I honestly haven't been able to. This is the first letter I've been allowed to write and will probably be the only one for a time so please be patient and don't worry. I'm safe and well so there is no cause for worry. We received our first mail in some time yesterday and yours of June 6 was among them. I also received the first copy of the newspaper [The Recorder] *but no packages. . . . Have been attending Mass and receiving Communion daily as we have the Catholic Chaplain with us. I thank God for that opportunity. It's a great help at a time like this. My love to all and regards to Dez. Please continue to write and be patient until you hear from me.*

All my love
Bud

Don't worry.

Pvt. Theodore Demanski, June 13, 1944, France; Pvt. Thomas Cronin, June 25, 1944, Normandy; Sgt. George Brown, July 6, 1944, Normandy; Pvt. William Hutchinson, July 27, 1944, France.

Lt. Lewis Di Leillo, October 4, 1944, France. "Missing, presumed dead, after leading a rearguard action to protect retreating troops." The presumption proved to be correct.

Remarkably, I attended Lt. Di Leillo's funeral several years ago. What a strange thing, indeed, to be about forty years old and participating in the last farewells of someone who had died in his early twenties nearly eight years before you were born. What a miracle that they had found his body, at last, and brought him across the sea to Amsterdam, to St. Mary's, where crusty old veterans lined up in solemn salute to their fallen, forever-young comrade.

The reading at his funeral service was from Deuteronomy 30:4: "Though you may have been driven to the farthest corner of the world, even from there will the Lord, your God, gather you; even from there will He bring you back." ৲

Reclining Memories

by Vanessa K. Mullins | *Milan, Michigan*

LIVING IN A SMALL TOWN like Milan, Michigan, can be quite boring, especially when the weather is nasty and young children are forced to stay indoors. On one such day, my seven-year-old daughter found our camera and pretended she was a famous photographer, snapping photos of anything that caught her fancy. I walked behind her, proud as a mom could possibly be, because I didn't have to tell her which button to press or how to aim the camera. She had obviously picked that up by herself from watching us take photographs.

As her adventures took her from one room to the next, she eventually found her father asleep in his recliner in the living room. He was picture perfect: footstool out, head back, mouth open—his 6'5" frame stretched out and relaxed. She stood at the end of the chair, near his feet, and like a seasoned photographer, eased down the button.

This one simple act—a little girl wanting to capture the image of her sleeping daddy—brought back a special evening from my own childhood when another little photographer took what was very nearly the same photo.

More than thirty years ago, my family lived in a two-story home similar to the one I now live in. In our basement, we had a large television—probably only a twenty-five-inch screen, which is small compared to some models today, but big to a little girl of six. Also in the basement was my dad's brown leather recliner. I imagine this was his haven from work and from his two rambunctious children.

On this particular day, Mom, my little brother, Jimmy, and I had just returned from the store where we had purchased a brand-new Polaroid Instamatic camera. I don't remember exactly where Jim was, but when Mom and I went searching for Dad, we found him asleep in his favorite chair. Silent as a mouse, Mom took a picture of him, then put down the camera. Dad woke while we were still waiting for the photo to develop. As my parents began to talk, not paying attention to me, I picked up the camera and moved to the end of the recliner, aiming it at my dad. I wanted to show him that I could do it, too.

Dad looked at my mom. "She's pointing it at my feet." My mom replied something about letting me take it anyway. He agreed and I did.

I held on to the slippery white bottom, waiting for the first picture I'd ever taken to develop. I watched and watched and finally, I could see Daddy's face, his green shirt and brown pants, and his favorite chair. It wasn't a picture of his feet, he was all there. And it was clear. I vividly remember the "I told you so" feeling. When I showed the picture to Dad, he was surprised but happy that it had come out perfectly.

But things aren't always picture-perfect in life. Within the year, my father became seriously ill and was hospitalized. I didn't know what was wrong with him, I just knew my brother and I weren't allowed to visit him in the hospital and he was there for a couple of months. Several times a week he called and talked to us, but never for very long. I don't remember much of the phone conversations, but I do remember the sound of his voice when he said he loved me. It was the last thing he ever said to me.

I don't remember much about my dad, just a few bits and pieces and flashes of wonderful memories. Even the ordinary things, such as the gentle swat on the bottom that he gave me for jumping on my bed, are now extraordinary in my mind. But that's okay. It's what I need.

In my mom's photo album, the Polaroid still sits among other pictures of my childhood. Almost every time I visit her, I look at the picture and remember my dad and that day. I hear his voice and see him in my mind exactly as he was then. Exactly. That was the day I showed my dad I wasn't a little girl anymore, and he was happy.

I often wonder what he'd think of me now. ॐ

The Mystery Rider

by Michele Deppe | *Salamonia, Indiana*

EVERY PASSING AUTUMN brings to mind my exhilarating ride down Main Street in Salamonia, Indiana, when I rode as the Headless Horseman. My favorite summer treat was visiting my cousin, Theresa, at her expansive Indiana dairy farm. I loved running out to the barn to welcome a dewy newborn calf, filling a basket with vegetables from the black earth of the garden, and listening, mesmerized, to my Uncle Ben's stories, told over huge bowls of vanilla ice cream. Cousin Theresa and I rode her two horses from sunup to sundown, spinning imaginary adventures, as we followed the winding trails through the tall woods by the pond.

Theresa was proud of her lanky sorrel mare, Ginger, and she was the only equestrian for miles who had a complete English riding habit and a proper English saddle and bridle to match. Everyone else in that little hamlet in Jay County rode Western, like a community of cookie-cutter cowgirls. My cousin dreamed of riding in the town parade, exuding a regal presence, outfitted as a "British rider."

Unfortunately, our plans for riding in the parade were doomed when my mount, Molly, came up lame. Molly was an elderly

Appaloosa mare who was flashy, in her coffee-colored coat with a blanket of splotched cream spilled across her rump. I imagined making an Indian costume to complement Molly's native good looks. But now Molly's lameness would reduce me to a foot-sore nomad, trailing my foxhunting cousin.

We set out to beg various neighbors for a loaner horse and were offered only Bill, a small pony with a dull pewter coat and a coarse black mane and tail that protruded in all directions. Bill was difficult to control and had a hard, bouncing gait. Despite his modest stature, he went everywhere with the urgency of a bullet.

Amazingly, Bill's owner dug out an old, parched-leather English saddle and bridle from his tack room to send along with us. Theresa looked forlorn for a moment, 'til I assured her that I would rather ride Bill bareback than steal her thunder as the only person with an English saddle! She brightened immediately and said that we would come up with a costume that would be perfect for me.

Bill pranced all the way home like a frantic racehorse. He whinnied loudly, shook his head, and pawed the ground like a maniac. I was embarrassed by his boisterous voice, and self-conscious that my long legs hung past his round belly.

Back home, we perched in the hayloft to brainstorm ideas for my parade costume. Studying the clothesline strewn with freshly washed linens below, I suddenly had an epiphany.

"What if I took the sheet, draped it over my head, and went as the Headless Horseman?" Theresa stared at me, her eyes growing wide with admiration at my idea. "Then," I continued, "no one would see Bill's English saddle, and his neighing would just add to the excitement of my character!"

Theresa and I raced down the hayloft ladder and dashed to the clothesline, where she began unpegging a dazzling white bedsheet. I turned my cowboy hat halfway around my head, so that the brim would create "shoulders" underneath the sheet, giving me the appearance of being headless. She adjusted the sheet so that the base of my cowboy hat was in the center.

"Oh, my," she said appreciatively, "you look really good. But, you need *blood* where the sheet sits on your hat!"

"Yeah!" As Theresa raced into the house to get a bottle of ketchup for my "stump," I giggled beneath the sheet and stamped my boots in glee. We also decided that we had better cut eyeholes in the sheet so I could see where Bill was taking me. After a half hour of begging, Aunt Beth gave us permission to go ahead and cut out the necessary peepholes.

Parade day finally came, and Bill was charged by the activity and music. Try as I might to keep him in line, Bill danced wildly all over the place behind Theresa and Ginger, snorting and squealing. Through my sheet, I could see a partial slice of the audience lining the sidewalks, and knew that Bill and I were creating quite a stir. I had the reins in my right hand and a plump jack-o'-lantern in the other, which I held on my flattened palm as proudly as a butler carrying a silver tray. I wore a white cardboard sign around my neck to clarify that I was, indeed, "the Headless Horseman."

As the parade drew to a close, the "Headless Horseman" was summoned to appear at the announcer's stand. Nervously wondering why the parade officials wanted to talk to me, I headed in the general direction and was greeted by the announcer, whom I saw flash by through one hole. He coaxed the pumpkin from my grasp and replaced it with a heavy object.

To my surprise, Bill and I had won second place in the costume competition of the parade! As we trotted away with the foot-tall wooden-based trophy, the crowd cheered, and Bill shrieked, perfectly convincing in his role as a mentally disturbed equine from Sleepy Hollow. Photographers snapped our picture for the newspaper. I was mistaken for a local junior 4-H champion, and my true identity was never revealed.

The trophy was grand. On the top was a gleaming rider jumping a horse over a large stone wall, and at the base, a nameplate to commemorate the event.

Although I'll always remember the ride, I'd long since forgotten the trophy. This spring, I discovered the lackluster old prize in the attic. I was surprised that the figure of horse and rider had decayed so much, but had to laugh in spite of it, for in a fitting tribute to the Headless Horseman, the rider's head had parted from the shoulders and rested in a poof of dust on the floor.

The Undiscovered Classic

by Emmy Lou Nefske | *Mackinac Island, Michigan*

THE SHINY BLACK WHEEL behind the curtain seemed to be calling her name.

Hey Leigha, remember me?

Leigha slowly peeled the dull curtain aside and coughed, partly because the dust on the garage curtain had become airborne, but mostly out of utter astonishment. Could it be her bike?

We've all experienced a moment in our lives when time seems to halt in our honor. That crystal-clear moment when rational thought is tossed aside, a million illogical notions rush through the brain, and silly ideas don't seem so silly anymore. For that brief instant, desires become actualized.

Leigha found herself immersed in this type of lucid dream that hot summer day in her friend's dingy garage.

Leigha was only seventeen. Not yet a senior in high school but already running from her suffocating hometown, she had spent the previous summer on the colonial haven of Mackinac Island, Michigan. Small towns have a way of molding you—without your consent—long before you have a chance or even a reason to think otherwise. So, in a time when other kids her age were reveling in what could be their last hurrah as high schoolers, Leigha was taking the first steps off the Arnold Line ferryboat and into a new world, looking to find herself.

When Leigha was a small child, in the days prior to her parents' divorce and her father's absence, she had spent endless hours in the family garage, assisting her papa in his motorcycle rebuilding endeavors. They shared a special bond: a love for free-spirited transportation. The historical nature of Mackinac Island prohibited motorized vehicles, but for as far as Leigha could see were the next best thing—bicycles of all varieties. Bikes lined the streets of her new island home, leaned against fully bloomed lilac bushes, waited patiently outside modest fudge shops. Moving through the crowded streets, she cautiously eyed shiny mountain bikes, beat-up tandems, and children's Huffys with banana-shaped seats, and brightened with pride. No one had a bike like hers.

Earlier that spring, Leigha's Aunt Pam had found the garage-sale dream. It was a Schwinn from the late 1950s, early '60s. Cherry red with black handlebars, a thick black bouncy seat, shiny silver fenders, and wire saddlebag basket. The bike was by no means a throwaway—it even had a bell. In elaborate, white cursive letters painted flamboyantly across the frame were the words HOLLYWOOD CRUISER. It was a classic, and Pam didn't hesitate in her purchase.

Leigha and her aunt were close—both shared an easygoing attitude—and when Pam offered the bike as island transportation, Leigha happily accepted. It was the Harley Davidson of bicycles, and Leigha immediately felt a surge of pride at the prospect of riding such legendary transportation. And ride it she did.

In good spirits, Leigha cruised with companions, singing the oldies and ringing her bell at just the right parts. She talked to the Hollywood Cruiser as if it were alive, and finally began to see herself in the same light. Like herself, the Hollywood Cruiser was a classic waiting to be discovered and spoken to without predetermined opinions. On somber days, Leigha rode her bike to the opposite side of the island, away from the bustling tourists. For hours she sat on the rocky shore of Lake Huron, gazing at the slow-moving barges on the blue horizon, wondering if her papa was a passenger, wondering if he thought of her, and if so, *what* he thought of her.

But nothing lasts forever, and one tragic day that summer, Leigha awoke to discover her bike was gone. She searched the streets, checking every Schwinn she saw, searching for the Hollywood Cruiser logo she had grown to cherish. As the search continued, she toyed with the idea that the bike had vanished, possibly ridden away on its own, anything but the brutal reality that someone had stolen her classic. Exhausted and heavy-hearted, she finally retired to the large Fort Mackinac lawn overlooking the bay and cried. She cried for the lost cruiser, she cried for her lost father, she cried for her lost identity.

A year later, Leigha wiped a single teardrop from her cheek and then shook the memory away. The bike behind the curtain was the same Schwinn, in green, but without the frills that had made her Hollywood Cruiser the classic it had been.

"I'll buy it from you," she offered, but immediately sighed in resignation. In her heart of hearts, she didn't really want it. The Hollywood Cruiser was gone, never to be replaced. And as that realization came to mind, another thought occurred. During the time the Cruiser had been hers, it had taught her the potential of undiscovered classics. Somewhere along the windswept shores of Mackinac Island, squashed in between the tourist-filled fudge shops and horse-drawn carriages, Leigha had learned that life goes on whether you're riding a Harley Davidson, a Hollywood Cruiser, or standing on your own two feet.

Whatever it was she was fixing to become would be great, because just like the Hollywood Cruiser, she now knew that she, too, mattered. ᘏ

Mackinac Island, Michigan

Population: 523

Scenic Isle

*I*n 1875, Mackinac Island became the nation's second national park, and in 1895, Michigan's first state park. Today, Mackinac Island State Park covers more than 80 percent of the island. More than 600 horses are stabled on the island during the summer months, and about twenty draft horses stay on the island during the winter months to provide service to the community.

In the winter, once the straits freeze over, Mackinac Island residents are provided with a natural ice bridge to the mainland. To help people keep their bearings, discarded Christmas trees are strategically erected in the snow, on top of the frozen water, serving as a much-needed guide for snowmobilers when the wind and snow sweeping across the ice turn the whole world white. ∾

A Sacred Place

*T*he island's Native Americans believe Mackinac Island is a sacred place and home to Gitchie Manitou. Because of its location in the center of the Great Lakes waterway, it became both a tribal gathering place where offerings were made to Gitchie Manitou and the burial grounds for many tribal chiefs. The name Michilimackinac, Land of the Great Turtle, was given to the island because its shape resembles a turtle's back. ∾

Town Facts

First incorporated • The village of Mackinac Island was incorporated in 1817. By 1818 it served as the seat for the territorial county of Michilimackinac.

Transportation • In 1920, an ordinance was drawn up that prohibited the use of motor vehicles, excluding emergency vehicles, on Mackinac Island. Since bicycles and horse-drawn carriages are the only forms of transportation, the island is enveloped in a nostalgic Victorian atmosphere that draws tourists from around the world.

Location • Mackinac Island, located on Lake Huron, is known as the Crown Jewel of Michigan. Tucked in along Michigan's silver coast, the island—4.4 miles across and 8.2 miles around—is easily accessible by ferry. In peak season, ferryboats make the fifteen-minute trip to and from the mainland every thirty minutes.

Places of note • The Grand Hotel, built in four months, boasts 385 guestrooms and a 660-foot porch—reputed to be the longest in the world. Two well-known movies were even shot there: *This Time for Keeps* and *Somewhere in Time*. The Devil's Kitchen, a limestone cavern created by erosion and the displacement of rocks due to cedar roots, can be seen from ferryboats approaching the island. Arch Rock rises nearly 150 feet above the water, on the island's east side. According to Anishinaabe-Ojibwe tradition, Arch Rock is the place where the Great Creator blew the breath of life into the newly created earth, and is the gateway through which the Great Creator passed on his way to Sugar Loaf, his island home.

Industry • The island's industry has progressed from fur trade to fishing, and since the Civil War, tourism. Special events that promote tourism include the Lilac Festival, the Port Huron Bayview Yacht Club's Race—generally referred to as the Port Huron to Mackinac race—and the Chicago Yacht Club Race to Mackinac.

A Gift from Mother

by Pat Capps Mehaffey | *Hamlin, Texas*

WITH DREAD, I ANTICIPATED THE FULL BLAST of dry, body-baking heat in the attic. Already, I felt it escaping down the stairway as I climbed the narrow steps. July 1960 was unusually hot in the small, west-Texas town of Hamlin.

Slitting the strapping tape on the first dusty box, I remembered when I packed, labeled, and stored the boxes in the attic on a cold, snowy day in 1952. Mother had died a few weeks previously and her house had to be emptied because the new owners wanted to move in immediately. I gave the tools, furniture and furnishings, and clothing to the appropriate people to be cherished and enjoyed, or maybe not, as they chose. The remaining items had no monetary value, yet Mother considered them her most treasured keepsakes.

I packed quickly on that long-ago sad day, only glancing at the diaries, birthday and Mother's Day cards, letters, telegrams, newspaper clippings, delicate handkerchiefs, and gloves. Mother didn't feel properly dressed unless she wore a hat and gloves and carried a hanky in her purse. Struggling with tears, I had moved all of her treasures out of sight.

Now my three nieces planned to arrive soon for a visit and I wanted to share Mother's treasures with them. At last, after all these years, I felt emotionally strong enough to examine each item and read each word of correspondence. Many of the cards, letters, and clippings pertained to my nieces' families. I knew each one would find special pleasure in reading them, and in having some of their grandmother's gloves and hankies.

Parting the cardboard flaps, I reached for the first tissue-paper-wrapped object, and memories rushed to my mind as I held up a pair of barber's scissors. The eight-inch blades were still the same cold, blue-black steel, but Mother's fingers had worn away most of the shiny coating on the handles. By angling them to the light, I could still read the words "Simmons-Howe Co., Inc.—Germany."

Recalling with clarity how Mother had valued her special scissors, a longing for days past drifted over me. With great pride, Mother often said that these scissors were a free gift when she and Daddy purchased a Home Comfort Range in 1928. She cherished the stove, too, but that had come with a price tag.

Sitting on the floor among the boxes, I clearly saw Mother on Saturday evenings cutting Dad's hair, my brother's hair, giving haircuts to the seasonal hired hands, neighbors, and anyone else who asked for cuts or trims. Several had beards, which she also shaped. My nieces and I wore Buster Brown haircuts with bangs straight across the forehead and Mother fretted that the bangs grew too fast even though she cut them very short.

One day, when I was about eleven years old, my nieces' fast-growing hair and Mother's special scissors combined to ensure I received a spanking. Often, I had observed Mother as she cut my nieces' hair. Confident I knew just how to do it, I draped an old sheet over each of my nieces' shoulders in turn by age and cut everyone's hair really short, thus saving Mother a lot of time and trouble. For some reason, Mother did not appreciate this act of kindness. In fact, she promptly went into what can only be described as a "fit."

Another vivid memory was the day Mother caught me using the scissors to cut out paper dolls. She delivered a long lecture about how cutting paper dulled the blades and we must never ever use the hair-cutting scissors to cut paper.

Occasionally, the scissors disappeared and everyone was enlisted to search and not stop until they were found. We all swore our innocence. Thankfully, the scissors were always found again.

Mother spent her last few years as an Alzheimer's patient. As the disease advanced, she lost the ability to speak in complete sentences. She no longer remembered nouns. Yet, even after she reached that stage in the advancing disease, she still asked for her scissors by opening and closing two fingers in a snipping motion.

Recovering from my reveries, I unpacked all the boxes, making a stack of memories for each of my nieces and one for myself. I tried to return each item to the rightful owner and divide all the treasures equally. Guess which of the stacks received the scissors?

Yes, I still have them. Mother's cherished barber scissors received many years of use, and I have plenty of practice with three little girls of my own, whose bangs grow very fast.

The Table Traveled Home

by Joyce McDonald Hoskins | *Clarksburg, West Virginia*

M<small>Y</small> F<small>ATHER</small> was a good man. He loved children, animals, and the outdoors. He worked hard, as men who grow up in small coal-mining towns in West Virginia still do. No job was physically too hard for him. He worked in the coal mines and later in a tire shop. He could lift me onto his shoulders with one hand. As a child, I was convinced he could carry a ton. Shooting a deer and carrying it back to camp was no problem for him. Considered a good marksman by the Clarksburg locals, he usually took first place at turkey shoots. He understood about things like fishing, hunting, and nature.

What Dad couldn't do was fix things. He wasn't the kind of dad you carried broken toys to because you knew he could fix anything. He could fix nothing. Nothing. Wiping away my tears to fix my broken heart was about all his big hands could manage.

He also could not make things. My dollhouse was store-bought. He might have said he built my brother a go-cart, but I suspect he paid someone to build it for him, and then slipped it into the garage on Christmas Eve.

No, Dad was not a handyman. He had all of the tools, but he would never admit to being clumsy with them. He would try, but the curtain rods were never straight, the shelf simply didn't stay on the wall. Mom finally gave up asking and found someone else to do her handyman stuff.

What I remember most about Dad was his genuine love for other people. He put others first. Even cancer couldn't take that away from him.

The last memory I have of my dad is talking to him on the phone from my home in Florida a few days before he lost his battle with cancer. His last words to me were "Honey, do you need anything?"

Had I answered yes, he would have moved heaven and earth to see that I got it.

In 1984, before my plane landed in West Virginia, Dad went to be with his heavenly Father. He was sixty-five years old.

He didn't leave much in this world: a few guns, some fishing equipment, and Grandma's butter churn. My brother has the guns. I have the butter churn. Not much, as the saying goes, to remember him by.

Not that I need anything to remember him. I'll never forget the way he grinned and picked me up so I could find the surprise chocolate bar in his jacket pocket. The candy bar was always in the inside pocket, but the game was to look in all of the pockets before it was found. I'll never forget traveling home with two children of my own, and how the surprise chocolate bar magically appeared in the inside pocket, again. Who needs something to remember him by when you see his grin on your son's face? Who needs something to remember him by when you can still picture him driving his red pickup home for lunch, and stopping at the end of the driveway so you could jump on the running board and ride to the front door? I remember. After all, I have his worn flannel shirt to snuggle in on a rare cold Florida night.

Still, sometimes I couldn't help but think that it would be nice to have something that was uniquely his.

Many years after both of my parents were gone, and my own children were grown, I renewed a relationship with one of my cousins. We had been close growing up, but had not seen much of one another for many years. Wrapped up in careers, child rearing, and the busy years when there is never enough time, visiting cousins fell to the wayside.

The phone call to Alexis began as a family matter and proceeded to making plans to meet halfway between our Florida homes. Over a lengthy telephone conversation, we agreed we would get together at a mall for lunch.

"See you Saturday," Alexis said as we were ready to hang up. Then she added, "Oh, by the way, I have a table that belonged to your dad to bring you."

"A table?"

"Yes, he made it in shop class when he was in high school. Aunt Mabel had it. She kept everything. I'll tell you about it Saturday."

"My dad made a table and it's still standing?"

"Yes."

I laughed. "Dad wasn't very handy. It must be a funny-looking table."

"No, actually, it's a nice table."

The following Saturday I heard the story of the table as we ate lunch.

When our fathers attended Shinnston High School, in West Virginia, the boys made tables in shop class. Alexis had asked our Aunt Mabel for the one her father had made. She took the table from West Virginia to Florida, where it sat for many years in her apartment. One day while rearranging furniture, she turned the table over and found my dad's name engraved on the bottom. The next time she visited, she and her father went to Aunt Mabel's and found the table that actually belonged to her dad. Aunt Mabel had given her the wrong table.

It would have been a treasure to me even if it had turned out to be a misshaped, wobbly mess, but it turned out to be a well-made, sturdy table.

Today, the table sits in my office beside my computer. I can picture my dad, a young, good-looking lad with wavy black hair and his trademark grin, making the table.

The table traveled from his mother's house, to his sister's house, to my cousin's apartment, to my house. It made its way from West Virginia to Florida, where it now rests beside my computer holding copy paper, notes, and the telephone. On days when I am writing and the words come hard, it comforts me by being there.

It will sit beside me as long as I am on this earth, and maybe one day it will travel again. ❧

Dedicated to the memory of Frank McDonald (1919 to 1984)

As the Parade Passes By

by Kristine Ziemnik | *Chippewa Lake, Ohio*

EVERY FOURTH OF JULY, Chippewa Lake in Ohio has a big parade. The main street is lined with people who anxiously await the start, which is always at one o'clock in the afternoon. If you aren't where you are supposed to be by then, you are completely out of luck, because the street will be closed until after the parade.

I don't think I have missed watching this parade in all of the thirty-three years I have lived in this quiet little town. I always sit, dressed in a patriotic shirt and an old sailor hat I've had since childhood, and watch with wonder as the band plays and the colorful floats pass.

Whenever our precious flag goes by, held by one of our local veterans, I think back to another Fourth of July, in the 1950s.

I was eight years old. My brother Ron was born close behind me, and Larry was right after him. We were baby boomers. The houses in our neighborhood all looked alike because of the building boom going on in the suburbs.

All in all, we had a good life, and there were many children to play with in our neighborhood. And playing was something we did well. We could actually play in the street without worrying that a speeding car would hit us. We could stay out at night playing kick-the-can and hide-and-seek or just catching lightning bugs without worrying that some evil person might snatch us away.

One year, on the Fourth of July, we took our playing to a new level. My brothers and I had the idea that if we could get enough of our playmates together, we could form our own little parade and march up and down the streets holding the flag. And that's just what we did.

We ran to each of our friends' homes and called for them. "Oh Rick-key!" "Oh Rick-key!" It seems kind of funny now, but "Oh Rick-key" with the "key" held out long and loud got good results. Ricky magically appeared at the door every time we called.

"Oh Bruce-cee!" "Oh Bill-ee!" We moved down the street to each house, calling until we had about ten kids willing to join in our special parade.

We needed props, and somehow managed to coax our dads into letting us borrow their rifles (without the bullets, of course) because most of our dads were World War II or Korean War veterans. The carrying of rifles down city streets in this day and age would be a huge cause for concern, but back then no one worried. We even scrounged up outfits to wear and were proud to wear them in spite of the July heat.

Mine was just a sailor's hat. My brother had one also. But other kids had army shirts and we even had a few Boy Scouts in full uniform. We were quite a sight! The biggest boy in the group held Old Glory as we took to the streets.

We marched with a whole lot of enthusiasm, yet there was an air of seriousness about our adventure. We were on a mission and didn't mind marching on streets a bit far from home.

Even at that early age, we all knew what that red, white, and blue cloth meant to our country. Didn't we recite the Pledge of Allegiance

every day at school? Weren't our dads' military pictures on our man-
tels? Didn't Janice's dad have a leg missing, due to time spent in the
service?

I got the biggest thrill when we passed people working in their
yards or washing their cars and they stopped and clapped their hands
for us. Whenever anyone saluted the flag, our marching five- and
six-year-olds saluted right back.

I have never forgotten that day or the feeling of doing something special for my country. We were only children, but we were also
patriots in every sense of the word.

And that's what I think about whenever the flag passes by at our
annual Fourth of July parade. I stand. I clap. I cheer. I wave my old
sailor hat. And I remember.

The Mountain Rises Again

by Tony Lolli | *East Burke, Vermont*

EVEN NOW, YOU CAN STILL FIND the old Burkie Bear posters here and there around the village of East Burke, Vermont. Burkie, a smiling bear cub on skis, was—once upon a time—the symbol of Burke Mountain. There was a time, however, when Burkie's smile reflected lost confidence. And Burkie wasn't the only one feeling that way.

Whispered rumors started long before the public announcement. And with the onslaught of such talk, the town of East Burke hunched up its shoulders against the hard times it was sure would come. Burke Mountain was closing. Ski season was a major part of the economic engine that drove the village of fewer than 500 residents. The announcement of a public auction caused great concern among residents and merchants alike. Yes, the mountain had changed hands several times in the past, but this was a foreclosure and the thought of winter without skiing—in this skiing community—was frightening.

Local business partners Jody Fried and Billy Turner were not certain the loss of the mountain was preordained. They had an idea but needed a plan. Over the course of the next few months, they contacted potential partners in preparation for the auction. They also launched a publicity campaign to bring greater awareness to the public at large.

"For four weeks, I did nothing but promote this opportunity and try to interest others in developing a community-based ski area," Fried said. "I grew up as a Burkie Bear kid, skiing on this mountain, and I wanted the same thing for my kids."

Fried, Turner, and Ford Hubbard, a retired mountain operations manager, developed a business plan. It outlined their ideas for operating the mountain as a bare-bones public ski area. This was an important departure from past operations and different from typical ski areas.

Burke Mountain could not compete with the giant ski areas in Vermont and New Hampshire. East Burke was not rich with night-life or expensive shopping. In resort towns, real estate sales were the engines that drove economics, not the skiing operation. Skiing was often operated as a loss leader. What East Burke did have was the benefits of small-town life.

Burke Mountain's business plan would have to be different to be successful. Public skiing, not real estate sales, would become the focus. Burke's market niche would depend on the area's ability to sell small-town friendliness, something in short supply at many large resorts.

The auction was held, but Fried's group lost to an anonymous bidder. What the successful bidder intended to do with the holdings was unknown. Would he subdivide and develop the area? Would he log the mountain? Fried approached the bidder's agent and showed him their business plans. They talked about possible cooperation and Fried felt there was still a chance for public skiing at Burke.

The bidder's agent also approached the Burke Mountain Academy (BMA), the nation's first ski racing school. The academy's primary interest was in maintaining a training facility for ski racing, or it would have to move away from East Burke. The academy was wary about the risk of running a public ski operation, because it might create a financial burden for the school.

"Once we were able to discuss the financial aspects of running the public skiing operation with the bidder's agent and with Jody Fried, we began to feel more comfortable," said Kirk Dwyer, BMA's new headmaster. As a result, Burke 2000, L.L.C., was formed, and the bidder conveyed his interest to BMA. The academy would remain in East Burke and Burke Mountain would once again be open for public skiing.

There was, however, one small condition: the mountain would open for public skiing only if the necessary funds to cover expenses could be obtained in advance of the season. This would require selling 1,500 season passes: almost twice as many as in the previous year. Just to make it interesting, the passes had to be sold in the next six weeks to ensure enough time to prepare for public skiing. Could twice as many passes be sold in less than six weeks without lengthy promotional time? Some board members were skeptical.

It was time for a full-court press.

Following a public meeting, fifty volunteers from across a broad spectrum of the community came forward and conducted the sales campaign. Numerous services were donated in printing, radio and TV advertising, and graphic design. Free daily newspaper coverage tracked the season pass sales. A Web page was designed and donated. Public service announcements played on radio stations. Area merchants accepted posters for display in their shops. Thirty thousand publicity pieces were stuffed and mailed. Many radio advertisers concluded their own purchased airtime ads with a reminder to participate in the Burke Mountain season-pass sale. Auto dealers gave season passes with auto purchases. The local health club offered a month's membership to anyone who bought a season pass. Area employers offered a subsidy for employees to purchase passes. The list goes on.

In addition, virtually every operational need was obtained at a discount from local merchants who wanted to help save Burke Mountain. This assistance included discounted fuel oil, a reduced rate for electricity, use of a vehicle from an area dealer, and free sand for road sanding. Other cost savings were implemented so the mountain operation could become as lean as possible and still be efficient, as outlined in the original business plan. Everyone who could pitch in did so. In the final two weeks, a flurry of activity sent the number over the top and the 2001 season was assured.

With all the hard work, a little luck would be in order. BMA training began right on schedule, as did the public skiing. Apparently, the planets stayed in alignment because that year's snow was the best in recent memory, making it possible to attract many new skiers to Burke Mountain.

All those involved had good reason to smile and even Burkie Bear's smile seemed to grow in confidence. So much so that he was called out of retirement to once again become the logo for the mountain. ∾

Gramma's Ring

by Alice A. Mendelsohn | *Carbondale, Pennsylvania*

RECENTLY, WHILE FUSSING OVER the perfect accessory to wear for a festive occasion, I chanced upon a precious item that had once belonged to my grandmother. As soon as my fingers touched the bauble, sweet memories rose to the surface, and all thoughts, save those from my past, disappeared.

I grew up in the "family home" in the small mining town of Carbondale, Pennsylvania. It was a crowded house, filled with love and laughter. Not only did my parents and brother, Joe, live there, but a few other relatives did as well. The most important part of this household, and our mainstay, was Grampa. He, being the patriarch, was the only person to have his own bedroom, which was on the second floor and was referred to as the "front room."

Grampa had a hard-and-fast rule: each of us had to be responsible for our own belongings. He felt that everything should have a home and we should always put things away in their home. Someone was always asking, "Where are my keys?" or "Did anyone see my book?" or "Whose comb is this?" Grampa would say, "If it was put in its home you'd know where it was."

Every so often, Joe or I would be called upstairs to Grampa's room to bring him a newspaper or magazine. When that happened, we felt honored. Sometimes Grampa just wanted to share some small talk with us. Maybe we'd be lucky enough to be invited to sit and share cookies and milk as he read aloud some of the articles in the magazine.

I always felt special sitting next to Grampa on those two soft chairs to the right of the windows. Directly in front of the windows was a long table with a soft white runner. It set the scene for the beautiful Tiffany lamp. I felt cozy and warm as the sun radiated throughout the room.

One day, Grampa called down and asked me to bring his blue pants upstairs to him. Not wanting to get them dirty, I folded them over my arm. On the way upstairs, I heard a noise. It sounded like metal hitting the metal edge on the stair runner. I looked down and saw the gold monogram belt buckle dangling and took it for granted that was what I had heard. I continued up and gave Grampa his pants and went back downstairs.

Later that evening, the household was in an uproar. We all knew that everything in Grampa's room had a home and was always put back in that home when he was done with it. We heard Grampa hysterically shouting, "Where's the ring? Where's the ring?" We knew something dreadful had happened.

Gramma had been deceased for many years and Grampa always kept her engagement ring in his pants pocket—the pants that I had just carried upstairs. When I explained I'd heard a metal-hitting-metal noise on the stairs, everyone began searching frantically on the steps and in the hall below—everywhere possible. It was bad enough when Grampa got annoyed at us for losing something of our own, but losing Gramma's ring was unacceptable. It must have been my age, for I do not recall who found the ring again, only that it was thankfully found.

Grampa always told me when I grew up, I could have Gramma's ring. Her name was Anna, which is my middle name. Her birthday was in July, as is mine. Gramma's birthstone, the ruby, shone from the middle of a gold setting with tiny pearls on each side, and I couldn't wait for the day when it would belong to me.

By the time the ring was handed down to my mother, after Grampa passed, the stones had fallen out, so she had the center stone replaced with *her* birthstone, the amethyst. But because the gold was soft with age, the stones kept falling out.

Many years later, during a family Christmas visit, we exchanged gifts, and Mom gave me a separate gift. We had not talked about the ring in many years, but as soon as Mom handed me that tiny package, I knew what it was—and I cried. I knew that inside that little package was the ring, which was now mine as Grampa had promised.

I dried my eyes and, still shaking with emotion, opened the box. Sure enough, there was Gramma's ring. I put the ring on my finger and kept looking at it and crying.

On Christmas Day, I wore the ring, showing it off proudly, still with an occasional tear as I told the story of losing it when I was a little girl. The look of puzzlement in everyone's eyes was comical. One person finally asked, "Do you know that you've lost the stones?"

There I was with Gramma's ring on my finger—no stones, just the old gold band. I was so happy to have the ring that I hadn't even noticed there were no stones!

We have since added a ruby and pearls, and the ring is restored to its original state. It is as beautiful as the day it was given to Gramma, as precious as the day it was lost, and appreciated as much as the day it was found. ～

Letters from the Front

by Steven Manchester | *Westport, Massachusetts*

WHILE GOING THROUGH a cardboard box in the attic one day, I discovered a pair of old letters sent between my father and me. Born and raised in the small town of Westport, Massachusetts, I'd been stationed on the front line of life at the University of Massachusetts, Amherst, and was already well into my sophomore year of college before realizing I knew absolutely nothing about the opposite sex.

I'd just met Tonia Brightman and everything about her changed my way of thinking.

Although friends and family predicted she would be just another in my long line of conquests, Tonia had different plans. In one way or another, she'd cast a spell on this roaming bachelor and to everyone's shock, I dove headfirst into her cauldron.

On an immediate and desperate quest for understanding, I'd written home for reinforcements.

Dear Dad,

As always, I hope this letter finds you and Mom well. Things are good here at school and I have no doubt that English Literature is the perfect major for me. So, relax! Your investment is being well-spent.

Dad, forgive me for cutting to the chase, but I need help. I think I've finally met "THE ONE!" Her name is Tonia. She's beautiful and sexy, with dark hair and eyes to match. But the problem is—she's confusing the heck out of me. Every time I think I know how to act, I'm wrong. Every time I think I've reacted correctly, I'm wrong. I wouldn't ask if it didn't mean so much to me. I really do need your advice!

Love,
Steve

I still imagine that my father dropped the letter onto the end table, leaned back in his rocking chair, and placed both hands behind his head. With a mischievous smile, he undoubtedly pondered my quest into the unknown. Half of him probably felt bad, while the other half must have chuckled. Women could be a rough trip for sure, but my Dad always joked that there was no better ride on earth. He responded with love.

Dearest Steve,

First and foremost, your Mom and I are well and I'm happy to find you are the same. Also, you should know—no matter which path you choose, you'll always be a solid investment. With that said—on to the pressing matter at hand.

Steve, above all things, you MUST be yourself, both in action and reaction. If any relationship demands differently, then it is destined to fail anyway. So, be you!

The rest is not as simple, so bear with your old man and let's see if I can't shed some light on your wonderful dilemma. By the grace of your lovely mother, I have learned:

Women are creatures of the heart, not intended to be understood, just loved. Mysterious by their very nature, they reveal only what they wish, leaving the rest to the efforts of those who dare to explore them within. They live by their feelings, rely on their instincts, and wonder why their needs are not understood without their ever explaining them. But trust me Steve, there has never been a more beautiful creature made by the hand of God.

Intentionally or subconsciously, women will test your heart and constantly check its depth. They can easily detect wandering eyes or sniff out anything less than the truth—without even being in your presence. They only wish to be placed first, though they will never request it. They desire solid communication, but will rarely say it. And they only yearn for someone who will understand them completely, though they will never, ever show their entire hand, but what a wasted life, my boy, to never know their ways.

All women are maternal and protective, almost territorial, when it comes to those they love. They can break your spirit with a look, or heal your soul with those same eyes. There is no softer touch, nor destructive hands—depending on the circumstance. The truth is found more in what they don't say, than in what they will have you hear. And little things like flowers and poetry mean more to them than you could ever imagine.

Possessing such complexity, it is still the simple things that seem to make them smile. But oh, the incredible joys you can reap in return!

These beautiful creatures like to feel the safety provided by a man, though they will fight to retain their independence. They are compassionate and sensitive and though they desire the same from a mate, they are also attracted to the crude ruggedness accompanied by raw masculinity. I suppose mysterious is not the word.

Steve, as I sit here and write this letter, it has become comically clear to me that I know so very little on the subject you ask. So, it looks like the rest becomes your research project. Trust me, son, if Tonia is "The One," your assignment will last no less than a lifetime.

Love Always,

Dad

P.S. When and if you do find some answers, let me know. I've always been just as curious! ◠

Singing on the Front Porch

by Lynn R. Hartz | *Charleston, West Virginia*

OPEN STAGE HAPPENS ONCE A MONTH in my town and I almost always go. The men and women who attend bring their guitars and other instruments to sing and play during the evening.

One guitar looks exactly like one my father had. It belongs to our director, Ron Sowell. The guitar is traditional in style, but the modernized version has a plug for amplifiers, which my father's guitar didn't have.

As my eyes pass over the guitar, memories surface, connecting me to days long past. I remember my father and his guitar. I remember our front porch alive with music.

The hot summer sun began its descent over the crest of the hill, passing over the front porch of our house at noon, leaving the lingering heat on our shaded side of the valley. The year was 1955, and few people had air-conditioned homes or televisions, especially where I lived in Charleston, in the mountains of West Virginia. There were more people outside in the evenings than indoors. The inside of every house on the mountain felt like a sweatbox or a locker room right after a football game.

In the evening, our front porch was a favorite gathering place for the neighbors, probably because our porch was the largest around and there were always children playing outside. There was always something happening, and it was usually accompanied by the sound of music. I do not mean music from a radio. This was real live music with guitars and banjos and mandolins and harmonicas, with real people playing the instruments, and all the sounds that combine to make melodies come alive.

If it were cool enough, I accompanied my father on the piano and music poured from inside to blend with the music outside.

My father, Rich, as he was known to most people, was able to play any musical instrument that he could pick up, and some that he couldn't. His brother, my Uncle Bill, could play just as well and sometimes joined us on the front porch. Neither of them had ever had a music lesson of any kind. They could play and sing as well as any country music star from Nashville.

All my father had to do was walk outside with his guitar in hand and the neighbors would begin to gather on our porch. Even a large porch doesn't hold everyone, though, so soon the front steps would be full of people from toddlers to teens to those turning gray.

Dad would pick and play and start a tune and soon everyone joined in, singing the old melodies and hymns that seem to be long forgotten in today's world. Within moments, the singing could be heard from one end of the valley to the other, and those who hadn't come to our porch would sit on their own porches and listen. I could see the people on the porches across the hill as they pulled up their chairs and made themselves comfortable.

When sunsets disappeared, stars began to twinkle, and the air had a touch of a cool breeze, the singing quieted from the lively "Comin' 'Round the Mountain" to love songs like "Love Me Tender" and "Tell Me Why." The babies snuggled close to their mothers or fathers and soon fell asleep. The teenagers drifted into their own kind of melancholy, and the adults became misty-eyed. One by one, neighbors wandered to their own homes, and finally, my father would go inside and put his guitar back in the closet.

As we closed our day in song on our front porch, I went to bed feeling warm and caressed by the love of my family and the joy of friends.

Tonight, as Ron picks up the guitar that looks like the one my father had, he leads the people at Open Stage in one last "sing together" before the night is over. We sing and the memories of those long-ago days with my father and his guitar are re-created with the same feeling of warmth. Tonight, as the guitar is carefully put away and we say good night on the front porch of the church building where Open Stage is held, I feel the same loving caress and warm joy that accompanied my childhood nights, and know I am surrounded by those who love me.

The Talking Machine

by M. DeLoris Henscheid | *Blackfoot, Idaho*

EACH YEAR, OUR CHURCH SPONSORS an antique show where dealers bring their treasures, set up individual displays, and wait for the nostalgic customer to find the exact piece that reminds them of Grandma. My usual purchase is a vintage platter or kitchen utensil. But this year, as I browsed through the maze of temporary shops, my eyes rested on the very telephone that hung in the kitchen of Grandma Mary's farmhouse.

I hadn't thought of Grandma's "Talking Machine" for years, but as I stood there, staring at that large, brown-and-black wall hanging, sixty-eight years melted away. Suddenly, I was back in the small farming community that wraps along the shores of the Blackfoot River. That particular ribbon of flowing water, before it tumbles into the mighty Snake, defines the northeast side of Fort Hall, the Shoshone/Bannock Indian Reservation, on one side, and the village of Blackfoot, Idaho, on the other.

The distance into town—over roads of mud, snow, or sand— was not casually traveled in that era, and life could sometimes be very lonely for the women who lived in the farmhouses scattered throughout the hills. During the dark days of winter, spirits were especially pulled down, matching the moods of raging storms.

I recall a winter, back in the 1930s, when I was four. Grandma held my hand as we stood by the window and watched driving white winds skate across the river, gathering ice to blast the old junipers and frost the berries that trembled on their branches. We watched the demon wind, determined to cut us off from all the world by filling every path that led to barns, outhouses, and neighbors. When the howling wind rumbled down the chimney into the big black cookstove, Grandma shuddered and stomped her foot.

"Stop that darn noise," she commanded the ebony-and-silver servant that heated the house and cooked our meals with its roaring heart of fire. When she twisted a small silver knob that hung from the tall, round chimney, the rumbling stopped, but Grandma grumbled all the more.

"I need to listen to something besides howling wind," she exclaimed as she headed for the box that hung on the kitchen wall. Lifting one black cup to her ear with one hand, she determinedly cranked the wooden handle with the other. She put another black cup to her mouth and said some numbers into it, then waited for a ring. Sometimes the rings would be three shorts, sometimes two longs or two shorts and one long.

Usually Grandma ignored the rings—unless it was one long and two shorts, which meant someone was calling her—but on those drifting, lonely days, when a woman longed for the sound of something besides that of the depressing wind, every lady along the Blackfoot Hills welcomed the sound of that ringing machine.

Sometimes five or six women would simultaneously lift a black cup, connect it with an anxious ear, then breathlessly press lips into the mouthpiece and greet whomever was on the other line.

"Hello, Mary? Are you there?"

"Yes, it's me, Agnes," Grandma answered into her machine. "Who else is here today?" Then the excited chattering began.

Grandpa teased her when he came in from the cold. "That darned box is nothing but a gossip machine and it's strung together with wagging tongues," he exclaimed.

But I knew why Grandma called it her "party line." When she talked into it, she sounded happy like she did when, on less stormy days, all the women were together, bent over a quilt, and needles flew as fast as words.

It truly was a party line, and that old talking machine was the perfect hostess, answering the needs of winter-weary women with gifts of companionship and cheer. Best of all, it was the kind of hostess that sometimes talked, but mostly listened and listened and listened. ⎲

Blackfoot, Idaho

Population: 10,419

How Blackfoot Got Its Name

*T*he word *Blackfoot* originated in 1818 when a party of traders, employed by the Hudson's Bay Company, traveled from the Missouri River to the Columbia. Due to strife between Native American tribes, wildfires (reportedly started to smoke invaders out) had gotten out of hand and burned great expanses of country. Anyone walking through these burned-out areas arrived on the other side with blackened moccasins. The Hudson Bay party referred to the Native Americans they'd met on their excursion as the "Indians with the black feet" or the "Blackfoot crowd." The name now identifies the town, meadows, river, reservoir, and railroad switch station, a station that had once been referred to as Grove City. ∽

Legend Has It . . .

*A*ccording to Carrie Adell Strahorn, who published *Fifteen Thousand Miles by Stage*, spending one night in the town of Blackfoot in the 1800s was more than enough for her. Strahorn noted that the minute she and her husband stepped foot into town, they were assaulted by a volley of shots as shouting echoed through downtown. Townsfolk were used to this type of behavior, as it occurred regularly when the cowboys rode into town. Apparently to a cowboy, just about anything was acceptable—even riding a horse into the shops and saloon. T. T. Danielson, a local merchant who doubled as the postmaster, was not surprised by the antics of the boisterous men on horseback, but neither was he unprepared. Instead of demanding that the activity cease, Danielson created a win-win situation by constructing wide doors on both ends of his building. The boys rode in and rode right back out again, eliminating some of the destruction and at the same time still allowing the cowboys their fun. ∽

Town Facts

First incorporated • The town of Blackfoot was officially incorporated in 1901, but the town's roots go back to the fur trade, which thrived in east Idaho in the early 1800s.

Location • Blackfoot, framed by the great Snake and Blackfoot rivers and the Shoshone Indian Reservation, is at the center of historical corridors.

Places of note • A three-hour or less drive in any direction will take you to the Craters of the Moon National Monument, Sun Valley, Salmon—home of Sacagawea, the Native American who led the Lewis and Clark expedition in 1804, with her son, Jean Baptiste—Yellowstone and Grand Teton National Parks, or Salt Lake City. The historic Nuart Theater is home to The Blackfoot Community Players, who perform plays and musicals in the theater. A converted "southern mansion" is now the Bingham County Historical Museum.

Local attractions • Since 1902, the Eastern Idaho State Fair has been held here. The Potato Expo, a unique museum housed in the old Oregon Short Line Railroad Depot, built in 1912, showcases the world's largest potato chip, a Marilyn Monroe exhibit featuring the former movie star in a burlap potato sack, antique farm equipment, a potato signed by Dan Quayle, and the Blackfoot Chamber of Commerce.

Interesting Facts

- Bingham County produces more potatoes than any county in the United States, and Blackfoot, the county seat, is known as the "Potato Capital of the World."
- Randy L'Teton, model for the Sacagawea dollar, is from Blackfoot.
- Travelers who have passed this way include Lewis and Clark, the Oregon Trail pioneers, and the Hayden Geological Expedition, which camped on the banks of the Blackfoot River on the way to survey Yellowstone Park.

The Rocking Horse

by Marilyn Rodriguez | *Fairview, Kansas*

WHEN MY SON, DAVID, asked Santa for a rocking horse, I remembered the rocking horse my parents had given me and went in search of it. What I found in the attic was a different horse than that which I remembered.

Time had taken its toll on my childhood companion. Splits in the horse's wooden body, like gaping wounds, marred its shoulder and flanks. The real leather bridle, reins, and stirrup straps crumbled beneath my touch. The lamb's-fleece saddle was filthy and worn bare down to the hide. I gently rubbed away the dust on the horse's sweet face and the lifelike brown eyes looked at me just as they had done so many years ago.

Memories flooded my mind. This wonderful gray rocking horse had carried me on magic adventures to the Wild West, chasing a herd of wild horses, driving cows on a cattle drive. Most often, he was a thoroughbred carrying me to victory in the Kentucky Derby. My wondrous rocking horse encouraged my imagination and fulfilled my childhood dreams.

With disregard for the dust and splinters, I lifted the old wooden horse carefully in my arms and carried it out of the attic.

In my workroom, I lovingly cleaned away the years of accumulated grime and assessed the damage. I stripped away the leather straps, the saddle, the stirrups, the trim, and the remaining paint. With glue, wood filler, and paint, my rocking horse would be as good as new.

I poured hours into repairing, sanding, and painting, until the horse looked nearly new. Living in the small town of Fairview, Kansas, I had a hard time finding the needed parts to repair the horse, but I was determined to restore my beloved friend so I could pass the rocking horse on to my young son. I searched for the right leathers to replace the original and found what I needed at a saddle and leather repair shop. In order to replace the saddle, I salvaged the fleece lining from an old coat and tacked it in place with ornate upholstery tacks. The rocking horse arrived in my life with a mane and tail made of real horsehair and finding replacements proved difficult. Just when I'd given up hope, a friend came to my rescue and presented me with a bundle of multicolored strands from the tails of her show horses. Gray, shiny, and looking new, my rocking horse stood waiting for its next rider.

On Christmas Eve, my husband and I tucked presents under the tree. The last one was special. My beloved rocking horse stood in the soft glow of the Christmas tree lights, looking as shiny and new as the day my parents had given it to me.

My husband turned to me with a smile. "You did a wonderful job. David will love it."

Our impatient four-year-old was up at dawn on Christmas morning, anxious to get the festivities started.

"Get up Mommy, Daddy! It's Christmas!" he announced, tugging excitedly at the blankets. For an instant, he bounced up onto our bed, then turned and headed out the door, racing down the stairs ahead of us. With the speed of a galloping pony, David dashed into the living room and then screeched to a halt, staring.

"Mommy, Santa brought it!" he cried. "Santa brought my rocking horse!" For David, the magic ride had already begun. Before we could help him, he had climbed into the saddle.

I stood watching, tears blurring my vision, and wondered where the rocking horse and his imagination would take him. Would he be a cowboy, a knight astride his mighty steed, or a jockey winning a big race?

David loved the rocking horse, even after he'd outgrown it. But, like a fond memory, he passed it on to another child in our family. The memories remain with all of us lucky enough to have enjoyed that magical rocking horse, and I hope somewhere out there another child is climbing astride that same wonderful old rocking horse, riding into an imaginary world where anything is possible. ᥱᎧ

Going, Going . . . Gone!

by Lanita Bradley Boyd | *Portland, Tennessee*

STRIDING FIRMLY UP INTO THE STEAMING ATTIC, I regretted that this hot August day was my only chance to examine the items my grandmother was selling at auction in September.

The dusty, musty smell was intensified by the heat. I could hardly breathe, but I sat briefly at the dormer window where I'd hidden to read as a child, before deciding I'd better look around and get back to Grandmother and the coolness below.

Sadly, I decided Grandmother was right about the worthlessness of the items destined for the sale. There were endless bags of cemetery ribbons, broken straw hats, boxes of newspaper clippings, empty thread spools, and scraps of fabrics. The furniture I examined had never been of high quality; most of the chairs had broken rungs or seats missing. There was a battered rocking chair that looked quite old, the missing cane seat long ago replaced with a piece of plywood. Something about the rocker touched me, and I made a mental note to ask Grandmother about the chair before I left.

I found several old quilts and caressed their textured surfaces, puckered by the tiny stitches and many washings. I would treasure any of them. "Improved Ninepatch," "Dresden Plate," "Wedding Ring"—all were patterns I'd known and loved when I'd spent the night with my grandparents.

Next, I turned to the second room, which held what Grandmother said was "just trash." She and Aunt Lola Mae had determined that this pile needed to be taken to the dump, but they were going to let the auctioneer take a look before it was hauled away.

I was surprised to see another quilt piled on top of the junk. I picked it up gingerly. Dust flew from it and threw me into a fit of coughing. Wet from the heat, I took the tattered quilt and hurried down the stairs.

"Why are you throwing this quilt away, Grandmother?" I asked, as she rolled her eyes and shook her head.

"I can't believe you dragged that old thing down here!" she said. "That quilt's a mess. Renters during the war used it in that room up there because it was good and warm. I always hated it. Later, I used it as a dust cover. Look at how ragged it is on the edges! Why on earth would you bring that down?"

"I love the way it looks," I replied. "There's so much of this one blue with little sprigs of white flowers on it, and the way it's mixed in with the denim patches looks great. It's unusual to have so much of one fabric in a quilt this old. Usually your quilts are all different patterns and colors."

"That's because I made it from my Mother Hubbard! You know, Lola Mae was born the day after my sixteenth birthday. I knew right then and there that I never wanted to go through that ordeal again. The minute I was able to be up and about, I started cutting up that big old dress that I'd lived in for months. I cut it up and made a quilt out of it and swore I'd never have another child. I was a mess back then." She shook her head, remembering.

"Well, I'm glad she wasn't your last or I wouldn't be here today!" I said with a smile. Turning the quilt over in my hands, I added, "You know, you could probably get some money for this at auction. Made in 1912 is pretty old."

"Oh, no, I won't! I wouldn't want the neighbors to see that ragged thing and know it came from my house! If you want it you can have it, because I am not letting anybody hold up that old rag."

I folded the quilt carefully and then inquired about the rocking chair I'd seen.

"Now that's an old piece," she said, her eyes lighting up with the memories. "Your great-grandmother rocked your granddaddy in it when he was a baby, and I don't know how long she'd had it before he was born in 1882. I just know it's old. I imagine somebody might pay quite a bit for it."

"I'm sure they will," I agreed, thinking I'd ask my brother, John, to bid on it for me.

Though I had to return to my own home, which was in a different state, John assured me he would be at the auction to bid on some items that he wanted as well as two for me: the rocking chair and any one quilt. I had made it clear to him that he was to outbid anyone who tried to get the rocker, and that any quilt he could get would be fine.

A few days later, when the auctioneer began singing the praises of the battered old rocker, my brother jumped into the bidding. As the price neared $100, the bidding was narrowed down to John and two others. The auctioneer pointed from one to the other and the bids continued to mount. My sister-in-law, Liz, standing at the edge of the crowd, heard someone say, "That's the grandson there, bidding on the chair." There was a gentle buzz across the crowd as the word was passed from one person to the next.

"That's the grandson bidding."

"That's the grandson . . ."

Quickly, the competing bids stopped.

Puzzled, the auctioneer prompted the bidders. "What'll you bid? What'll you bid? You're not stopping now, are you? This chair is well over a hundred years old and somebody's getting a bargain here. Come on, now, one-twenty? Won't you make it one-twenty? No? What about you, ma'am? It's a steal for one-twenty! No?" He shook his head then raised his arm. "Going, going . . . gone! Sold for one hundred fifteen dollars!" And he slammed down his gavel.

John was as startled as the auctioneer that the bidding had stopped so early and abruptly, but Liz knew what had happened.

Today, I rock my granddaughter in the newly caned rocker in my kitchen and enjoy seeing the "Mother Hubbard" quilt, still tattered, spread over a round table in my living room. The quilt from the auction is perfect to provide warmth to my bed in winter, and all three treasures provide warmth to my soul year-round.

I smile now when I think about how disappointed the auctioneer must have been in the prices that some items brought that day so long ago. But if he'd watched closely, he'd have seen that the bidding always slowed down whenever "the grandson" started bidding. For neighbors in Portland, Tennessee, letting a grandson have a treasured piece of family furniture was more important than getting it themselves.

That's just the way things were done in Portland.

The Louisville Slugger

by Ray Weaver | *Pasadena, Maryland*

DAD HAD BEEN GONE for about a year, and it was time to clean out the rest of his things. My sisters were going to help Mom in the house—getting his clothes ready for the church—while their husbands and I went through the tools and assorted junk in his old shed. I am famously late for everything, but this time I got home a little before everyone else. I grabbed a cup of coffee, kissed Mom, and headed out back. I wanted a moment alone among the hammers, saws, jars of nails, torn-down lawn mower engines, and half-empty paint cans that still breathed the essence of the man who had been my father.

The door to the shed screeched in rusty protest as I pulled it open. It had never made so much as a squeak when Dad was still alive. He had kept it well oiled and was out in his shed nearly every day. He always had about ten projects going on at the same time that he was "just about finished with." Most of them were still there in his shed, still waiting to be finished.

I rested my coffee cup on a shelf, brushed impatiently at a tear, and got on with the sad business at hand. I tossed some of Dad's well-worn hand tools into an old toolbox so my brothers-in-law could sort through them later. When I saw his old Weedwacker back in a corner, I was sure one of the boys would want it, so I dug it out. There, hidden behind the oily, grassy whacker, was something that hadn't actually belonged to my dad. It was, in fact, mine. Still, it bound me to my father in a way that none of the rest of the stuff in that musty old shed ever could.

It was a Louisville Slugger. White ash. The black electrical tape Dad had carefully wrapped around the handle was unraveling, cracked, and peeling. There were scuff marks on the business side from the sweet spot to the handle, but precious few on the Hillerich and Bradsby trademark side, because every boy knows that hitting on the mark guarantees a broken bat. The "28" stamped on the knob at the bottom was nearly scraped away by the countless times it had been dragged across the sand of a Little League field or asphalt of a playground. I had started Little League with this bat and played with it for one or two seasons until both I and the bats got larger. In those later years, I became a pretty good ballplayer. But when I was seven years old and this 28-ounce stick had been my Excalibur, I suffered from the most terrible curse that can afflict a small boy.

I was afraid of the ball.

I loved baseball. My whole family loved baseball. Even my very strict grandfather, who didn't like us to read the funnies on Sunday, would let us listen to our beloved Orioles on the radio. I had ached for the day when I'd be old enough to join Little League. The day I got my first uniform, I stood in front of the mirror and admired myself for hours in my knickers, kneesocks, and shirt that had the words REBELS on the front and MEATS AND MORE on the back. Mom said I was going to wear my uniform out before I ever played my first game. Dad gave me my bat the day before my first game. I could already hear the *CRACK* it would make when I launched that very first Little League pitch into the stratosphere and served notice to everyone that I had *arrived*, baby.

I had always been a solid sandlot ballplayer. What I didn't realize was that by some cruel trick of my November birthday, I wouldn't be playing Little League with kids my own age. Because my birthday was late in the year, I wound up moving into the bottom of the age group above mine and playing with boys who were two and sometimes even three years older than me. They pitched hard. Really hard. Some of them could even throw the beginnings of a curveball, albeit not with much accuracy, and that was part of the problem. I did fine as long as the coach was lobbing fat ones at batting practice, but come game time it was a different story. I went from being one of the best hitters to cowering at the plate until three strikes were called; sometimes I even bailed out on a pitch right down the middle because I was convinced it was about to bean me. The Slugger never left my shoulder. I began to suffer that ultimate boyhood indignity of outfielders moving in and yelling "Easy out" whenever I stepped up to the plate. After every game, I sat in the back of the car, fighting back tears of shame. Dad would smile into the rearview mirror and say, "Don't worry. You'll get 'em next time." But I knew it wasn't true. I was afraid of the ball.

I started to hate baseball. I wanted to quit.

One Thursday evening before dinner, Dad had just come home from work and I could see he was tired, so the last thing I expected was for him to say, "Grab your bat and your glove."

We went out into the backyard and tossed the ball around a little bit. No big deal, we did that all the time. Then Dad asked, "So, how's it going at the plate?"

"You know how it's going," I mumbled. "I stink."

"No, you don't stink. You're a good hitter. You're just afraid of the ball."

"I am not."

"Yes, you are, and it's okay—even smart to be a little afraid. That'll save your butt. We just gotta get you over being so afraid that you won't stay in the box. Here, throw me the ball. As hard as you can."

Dad had his glove on, and was handy with it, so I didn't think anything of it when I whipped the ball at him as hard as I could. That is, until he dropped his glove, quickly stood up, and let the ball hit him right in the chest. He winced a bit.

"Wow, good arm. That one stung! Do it again," he said as he tossed the ball back to me.

I was stunned that he'd let the ball hit him and even more upset that he wanted me to do it again. I looked him straight in the eye and yelled back, "No way!"

"Ray, I said throw the ball," he replied in his most authoritative voice.

Boys in those days did as they were told, so I tossed an easy one in his general direction. He fired it back at me and said, "I said throw it. Hard."

So I let it fly. This time, instead of letting it hit him, he dropped to the ground and the ball sailed up and hit the side of the house. He stood up and waved as Mom's frowning face appeared in the kitchen window.

"See, son. I let one hit me, and it stung a little, but it didn't kill me. I kept my eye on the other one, and it never even touched me. I've been watching you. You close your eyes, just for a second, whenever the pitcher throws the ball, so you don't know where it is, and you get scared of it popping you. Now it's your turn. Just keep your eye on the ball."

(I am afraid that modern-day child psychologists will have heart failure at what happened next. All I can say is . . . relax. It was one of the best lessons I ever learned.)

My dad threw the ball at me.

He took away my glove and bat and whipped the Rawlings right at me. Never too hard, never too fast, but hard enough and fast enough that I had to dive to get out of the way and it stung like heck when I didn't move quite fast enough.

Yeah, it stung. But it didn't kill me.

I am not about to belabor the obvious analogy here, dealing with life and stuff coming at you and learning when to duck and how to take the hits when they come. You'll have to figure that out on your own.

What I learned that day was how to stay in the batter's box and keep my eye on the ball. While some might say it was nuts to throw a baseball at a small boy, my dad knew it was much harder on me to constantly fail at something I loved so much.

He had no intention of hurting me—he was teaching me, and sometimes, hard lessons can only come the hard way. Maybe his methodology wouldn't pass muster in these more "enlightened" times, but let me simply say this: it worked.

By the time Dad let me have my bat back in the twilight of that Baltimore evening, he was bringing the heat, and I was spraying it all over the yard. Our old house still has some broken shingles to prove it.

My first at bat at the next game, I swung on the very first pitch and launched it. It didn't quite make the stratosphere; in fact, it barely cleared the second baseman's head. When the dust cleared, however, I was standing on first base. I looked for my dad in the wooden stands, and he smiled. Nothing I have ever accomplished since has made me as proud as that bloop single up the middle. Nothing.

When my brothers-in-law finally showed, we finished cleaning out the fragments of one man's life. They asked me what I wanted before they divvied up the rest. I told them they could have it all.

Everything except one 28-ounce piece of wood. ⟳

Pickled Beets

by Shauna Smith-Duty | *Lawton, Oklahoma*

ON OCTOBER 16, 1974, my grandpa planted a weeping willow tree on the front edge of his backyard garden in Lawton, Oklahoma. It was the day I was born. I like to think he planted it there so that when he turned over his trashcan and plopped his spindly frame down for a rest, stretching out those long, skinny legs of his and wiping his brow with a handkerchief, he'd catch a glimpse of the tree and think of me.

I think of him often. He was quite a man. His blue eyes sparkled when he laughed, and he laughed a lot. He smelled like Old Spice and fresh soil. He had a piece of iron embedded in his hand from knocking two hammers together in his youth. I was amazed by that story. After hearing it, I never, ever knocked hammers together!

I remember him asking me if I wanted a chocolate malt once, and his shock and dismay when I said I'd never had one.

"Why," he said with a long, drawn-out syllable, "you've never had a chocolate malt? I can't believe your parents never got you a chocolate malt!" It was as if they had neglected me since birth.

I saw my opportunity to milk the situation and still give my parents some credit. "Well, I only ever had a shake," I pouted as I shook my head, pigtails bouncing.

He smiled. "Sweetie, I'm gonna buy you a chocolate malt." He ordered me a large. I loved it.

He's the only one who ever called me Sweetie. At the time, there were two other grandchildren close enough to visit, and he babysat them regularly. Seeing them daily, and seeing me rarely, he called *me* Sweetie. They were Mop Head and Toe Joe. It still makes me feel special to think about the love he and I shared.

Though I miss seeing him, I sometimes catch a glimpse of him in my father's eyes or my brother's smile.

Grandpa was always known in his family and community as a gardener. He came from Oklahoma blood and grew up on a farm. A sodbuster through and through, he was probably working the land as soon as he could hold a spade. His garden was beautiful every year. Straight rows of cornstalks stood like tall soldiers in the sun, producing sweet ears of golden corn for our dinner. The man had a dry sense of humor and a green thumb. Huge tomatoes, mountains of okra, green beans, squash, and beets filled the kitchen all summer long. There was so much that he and my grandmother canned and froze food for weeks. Our household got a good share of that wonderful produce, and I am ever thankful for it. The flavor of his pickled beets lingers on my palate to this day. It was just a backyard garden, but it was his joy.

Hours upon hours of his life were spent painstakingly working the land and manipulating the plants for the best results. He watched the clouds for weather changes and knew all the gardener's secrets for getting rid of pests and producing a prime, succulent crop.

I remember Grandpa talking over the fence with his neighbor and friend, Mr. Martin. I don't recall being within earshot of any of those conversations, and with Grandpa's sense of humor, that was probably for the best. I stayed in my willow tree, watching Grandpa and Mr. Martin from afar, wrapping the spindly, dripping branches around my body and winding myself up like a yo-yo, then letting go and feeling the arms of leaves unravel to leave me standing in the hot summer sunshine.

Near the back of Grandpa's garden was the pear tree. If I was lucky, Grandma would have enough time to create her delicious pear cake before I headed home to Texas. To this day there is not a pear cake on the face of the earth that compares to hers.

In his later years, Grandpa teased us about his ability to continue gardening. "Well," he'd say, his blue eyes sparkling, "don't think I'll plant next year. Just too much! I'm getting on and can't keep up."

For years it was a standing joke. He'd make that same comment after fall harvest, and the next spring he'd put on his hat, throw a spade over his shoulder, and head out to the garden plot. We never took him seriously. With his sense of humor, who knew what to take seriously? We did notice that his garden was getting smaller each year, though. Then, one sad spring, he did not plant. I never thought it would happen, but in October of my twenty-fifth year, Grandpa passed on.

Passed on. What terminology. But, in fact, Grandpa did pass on. He passed on a love for feeling the cool spring soil between my fingers and a desperate desire to see new seedlings sprout, grow, and flourish in the summer sunshine.

I don't plant a vegetable garden like Grandpa's—nothing even close—but at least once a week I can be found bottom up and head down in my flowerbed. That's what he passed on to me—his joy of gardening.

One lone jar of pickled beets sits on a shelf in my curio cabinet collecting dust. Each time I look at the Kerr canning jar, I can taste the deep red beets so familiar to my mouth, but I just can't bring myself to open it. Upon closer examination, it's obvious that the beets are disintegrating. Soon they will be indistinguishable, and they are the only physical link I have to Grandpa's garden and to my grandpa. But I feel privileged to say that his joy does live on through me. ᏟᏅ

Open Windows

by Kim Ballard | *Smithfield, North Carolina*

MaRuth and Pa's house provided stability for my sister and me. No matter what part of the country we lived in, we knew every Christmas, one week in the summer, and maybe Easter would be spent in Smithfield, North Carolina. Their Cape Cod–style home, which Pa built for his bride in the 1920s, had wood-frame windows, painted white, with rope pulleys in the sides, and half-moon brass hooks to latch the bottom frame with the top.

The kitchen always seemed bright, though I know sunlight reached in for only a few hours each day. The windows had corner shelves between them and the cabinets. Miniature glass pitchers of different colors channeled sunlight in bright prisms across the room, while ivy from two small clay pots cascaded lightly down either side of the front window. When my mother renovated the house after MaRuth died, my grandfather having died a decade before, she gave me a window.

Now, when I look at that window, it's as if I could see back through time to every one of those wonderful childhood visits. During one memorable visit, my mama watched from the kitchen window and saw me do something she had expressly told me not to do. Lucky for me, Pa, my grandfather, came to my rescue. I was ten years old at the time and thought I knew everything.

While all of my cousins played outside, the women worked in the kitchen preparing dinner and the men sat in the living room comparing financial gains. I followed my nose. The smell of chicken pastry, creamed corn, and butter beans led me in through the kitchen door and made my stomach growl. It was at that moment that my mother caught me for a chore.

"Kimbo, I need you to run to the car and get my sandals from the floorboard in the back seat," she said barely looking up from her work. "Keys are in my purse over yonder, by the door, I think, honey."

The habit of living in larger cities meant locking the car door every time you left it, even when parked in the driveway, in a small town, where most people never even locked their homes.

I found the keys and bounded back through the house and out the kitchen's screeching screen door, across the yard, and stepped into view in front of the open window where MaRuth and Mama were working at the sink. The front yard had two pecan trees that framed the front corners of Pa's acre near the street. Two plum trees paralleled them on either side at the front of the house.

Crossing the front yard as I had a million times, I tossed the keys up into the air and caught them again and again. I had just thrown them as high as I could among the leafless branches when suddenly my mother's voice shot out the kitchen window, piercing the neighborhood.

"Kimberly Michelle! Don't you go getting those keys hung up in a tree branch! Stop throwing those keys, now, before they get stuck!"

"Don't worry, Mama," i called back without turning, knowing that it would be impossible to get the keys stuck on a tree branch. How absurd. So I tossed them again with confidence and arrogance.

And then it happened. I stood staring into the limbs, my stride broken by the interrupted moment that shifted my whole balance, expecting something to fall back into my hands that didn't. I could not believe my eyes. I knew Mama was watching me through the window and I was in big trouble.

"What did I just tell you, young lady?" Yep, she'd seen it happen.

Then I heard a wonderful, subtle, guttural laugh. Pa's laugh rang gently with sheer amusement. I turned to see him standing on the stoop outside the kitchen door, one hand in his pocket, the other holding a cigarette. He trotted down the three steps and across the shared gravel driveway to the neighbors' back porch and disappeared for a moment. I looked back up into the tree nervously. Mama was still speaking—but I had effectively tuned her out. How was I going to get those keys down? I could easily climb the plum tree—several branches were low enough—but not the tall, slender pecan tree.

Crunching steps caught my attention and I turned away from the tree long enough to see Pa reappear with a fishing pole. Without a word, he moved to my side beneath the tree, propped the cigarette between his lips, reached the pole up into the branches, and effortlessly pierced the key ring, pulling it until the keys fell off the branch. I thanked him profusely. He took the cigarette out of his mouth and patted my shoulder, still chuckling.

"Best mind your mama from now on," he said.

That was it. That and the sound of his retreating steps crunching on the gravel as he returned to the back of the neighbors' house. I am forever grateful that his intervention let me off the hook with Mama that time. His laughter and gentle reproof as he came to my rescue continue to lighten my spirit.

The last time I visited, I stayed, as always, in my uncle's old bedroom upstairs. The stairs were narrow, high, and hollow—made of wood, as were the walls on either side—and emanated their own special stain smell. Shuffle-thud sounds echo now in my memory as they had echoed in the house as windows were raised or lowered to accommodate the weather. The bedrooms were at either end of the house and the stairs opened into a small central play area. The bathroom was at the back of the house and had white tile, with a white porcelain tub, toilet, and sink with exposed pipes. There was no shower.

I loved bathing up there in the summer when I could open the window to feel and smell the fresh air that whispered through the thin white curtain and mingled with the fragrance of Ivory soap. One summer morning, a ladybug landed on the wide window ledge, just above the side of the bathtub. I watched it crawl across the sill, over the lip, down the wall, and onto the side of the tub. How marvelous the drop of dark red on the shining white porcelain! MaRuth had always told us that ladybugs were a sign of a healthy garden, and her garden and her home had an abundance of ladybugs.

Since my grandmother's death eight years ago, I have many reminders of her and Pa. I wear MaRuth's engagement ring, and I will always treasure the window my mom gave me. Whether it is the same window my mother looked through as I tossed the keys that day, or the one the ladybug flew in through, doesn't matter. What matters is that it is a pleasant reminder of who I am and where I come from, and I treasure it. ᑲ

Whistle Stop in Irondale

by Thelma Vaughan Mueller | *Irondale, Alabama*

IT WAS 1937. I had just turned eight years old and was going to camp for the first time. As an only child, the prospect of spending two weeks with built-in playmates set every cell in my body singing. A highlight of the trip would be my first train ride—twenty-nine miles to Eden, Alabama—where open-back trucks would haul us down to Kelly's Creek.

At 1:30 on a Monday afternoon, campers and parents deluged Birmingham's old terminal station. Some of the younger kids were clinging to their mothers. Several mothers, on the verge of tears, were hugging their kids. My mother quickly located a friend whose daughter had attended camp last year and with whom I was to sit.

Slowly, the train chugged out of the station and the old campers burst into song: "The dummy line, the dummy line. Ride and shine on the dummy line." The train whistle blew jubilantly as we approached Irondale, in those days only a railway switching center and a whistle stop, where a few more kids boarded the train, lugging their laundry bags stuffed with clothes and bedding. Behind the whistling engine, the joyful train continued to clack its way down the tracks toward Eden.

◄o►

In 1939, my parents and I boarded the train to New York for the World's Fair. The train rocked me to sleep, the sound of its whistle, the rhythm of the wheels on the track a lullaby.

At the fair, my mother bought me a small doll dressed in native garb at each foreign exhibit, ever connecting me with a wider world beyond.

⊘⊘

Several years later, my parents stood on the station platform, waving, as a train carried me from Alabama into my ever-expanding universe of college, then foreign service.

As an adult, I submitted to travel by plane, never feeling any excitement on those buses in the sky. Whenever possible, I rode the train back to Alabama. In my ever-pressured life, I could always relax on a train. The train accomplished the task of getting me from one place to another, and I was once again free to rest in the rhythm of its movement, the solo music of its whistle.

⊘⊘

My wandering over, I returned to Alabama, where my parents were aging. I bought a small house atop a hill, not five minutes from the retirement home where they lived. Signing the contract, I did not consider that the house lay adjacent to Irondale, which, in my years away, had grown into a small town on the outskirts of an ever-sprawling Birmingham. In a fitful sleep amidst unpacked boxes that first night, I heard the sound of a train whistle finding its way up the mountainside from the railroad tracks of Irondale. In the 2:00 A.M. darkness, I sighed contentedly, turned over, and slept peacefully.

Soon, two retired friends and I were driving twice weekly down into the valley below at lunchtime. In the heart of Irondale, we often found ourselves blocked at the railroad crossing by long freight trains, while friendly engineers switched them onto various tracks. On the other side of the tracks stood the Irondale Café, where we found the country-cooked fresh vegetables we craved.

In the late 1990s, the sleepy little community of Irondale suddenly became famous. The movie *Fried Green Tomatoes,* from a book by Birmingham author Fannie Flagg, had just been produced. It featured the "Whistle Stop Cafe," in truth the Irondale Café, which Fannie Flagg's aunt had operated from 1932, when it catered to railroad crews, until 1972, when hungry customers came from throughout the county. Before the movie, lunch lines had often extended out onto the sidewalk. Afterward, the line on the sidewalk frequently snaked past the corner and up a side street. Overnight, Irondale had become a tourist attraction. Basking in its newfound fame, the town of Irondale hauled an old locomotive onto a siding across from the café and polished it up.

Campers, often the granddaughters of my campmates, are now driven to Kelly's Creek on air-conditioned buses. Instead of scrambling up a narrow path to the outhouse, they use well-lit restrooms. They learn the dead-man's float in a chlorinated pool instead of the snake-infested creek.

My father lived to age 99, my mother to 101. During my mother's last years, I became aware that she was terrified I might abandon her to live again in Europe, or to teach in Hong Kong. Until then, I never realized the emotional cost exacted from her each time she encouraged me to board those trains so long ago. To my mother, the train's lonesome whistle is what had kept us apart, for it was the train that took her only child in ever-widening arcs away from her. Though she knew the train no longer stopped in Irondale, sometimes, late at night, the mournful whistle was a reminder of the times when it had. ⟲

THE TOWN OF

Irondale, Alabama

Population: 9,813

Famous Local Eats

The novel *Fried Green Tomatoes at the Whistle Stop Cafe* by Fannie Flagg was created around the Whistle Stop Cafe in Irondale. The movie, *Fried Green Tomatoes*, added to Irondale's popularity, and the tomato recipe from the movie has become popular all over the United States.

Founded in 1928 as a hot dog stand, the eatery used to be a stone's throw from the railroad tracks. In those days, Irondale reaped the benefits of its location between the freight yards of the Alabama Great Southern Railroad and the Georgia Pacific Company.

In 1932, Miss Bess Fortenberry took ownership of the restaurant and added to its menu. She and her friend Sue Lovelace and a cook named Lizzie Cunningham offered a host of home-style favorites. Soon, hungry patrons were lined up out the door. At that time, to-go orders were encouraged because the two dining rooms seated fewer than fifty customers.

When failing health caused Fortenberry to sell her business in 1972, she hired the McMichaels family to continue the café's traditional favorites while adding their own touches to the menu. The McMichael family took the little café from a seating capacity of 32 to 260.

After the movie came out, people came to the restaurant in droves, including tour groups and buses. At last count, its guest book included visitors from every state and thirty countries.

The current owner, Jim Dolan, remains true to Fortenberry's original vision by offering an array of home-cooked favorites, including 500 pounds of green tomatoes a week.

Though the area is no longer known as a railroad center, people still make tracks to Irondale. ❧

Town Facts

First incorporated • Irondale was incorporated on October 19, 1887.

Location • Irondale, nestled deep within a valley, is surrounded by mountains. Cahaba Mountain, or as locals call it, "Shades Mountain," lies to the south and Red Mountain (a place where Native Americans and early settlers found red clay worthy of face paint and cloth dye) to the north. Red Mountain, teeming with wildlife and panoramic scenery, is also known for its many streams and rivers. Additionally, it is rich in rock deposits, including limestone, iron ore, and coal.

Industry • Motion Industries employs approximately 200 people in its distribution factory. Its slogan, "Keeping industry in motion," is accomplished by distributing everything from bearings, seals, and sprockets to motors to larger factories.

Also located just outside of Irondale is the buyer's office of Books-A-Million, one of the largest book retailers in the country.

How Irondale Got Its Name

In 1863 W. S. McElwain of Holly Springs, Mississippi, built a pig iron furnace just outside the city limits of what currently is the town of Irondale. Pig iron produced at this spot was transported from Montevallo to Selma, where it was used to make weapons for the Confederate army. Two short years after the furnace opened, Wilson's Raiders destroyed the Irondale furnace in a senseless act of retribution. McElwain, ever the businessman, wasted no time in opening the furnace again, this time for farming equipment. Some ten years later, with the coming of the Great Depression and the Panic of 1873, the furnace closed permanently.

Though the furnace was originally called Cahaba Iron Works, townsfolk tacked on the nickname, Irondale, which is still in use today. ∾

Angela's Hidden Treasure

by Trish Ayers | *Berea, Kentucky*

WE PASSED THE HOUSE before we saw the sign tacked to the cedar tree. We were house hunting, and pickings in our little town were mighty slim. Some months earlier, the area had been hit by a tornado, which damaged more than 200 residences.

Seeing the words FOR SALE handwritten on that cardboard sign renewed our hope. We raced to our apartment to dial the phone number and within minutes were inside the white clapboard farmhouse.

The owner had been in the hospital for the past year and the house smelled of being closed up, but I saw past the smell and the dust and imagined the stories the house must hold. As if reading our minds, the elderly woman who owned the house invited us to sit down while she shared stories about the piles of treasures that surrounded her. There were oak chests filled with postcards from both World War I and II. She asked if we would deliver the chests to the special collections in the local college library, saying she felt the postcards should be shared with the world. We found ourselves agreeing, even though we had not yet decided if we would purchase the house.

When we returned home, I struggled to convince my family to look past the dust and muss. I reminded them the house was in a good neighborhood, mere blocks from the college and craft shops that made our town so special. I talked of the quaint window in the kitchen with screens that slid side to side. I joked, saying we could open up our own ice-cream shop and people could come to the window to place their order. Finally, they realized that any house was better than none.

But when we returned to tell the owner of our interest, the sign was gone! Afraid the woman had either changed her mind or sold the house already, we anxiously knocked on the door. She opened the door with a smile on her face.

With a conspiratorial wink, she confided, "After you left, I took the sign down."

But even so, in our small town, word travels fast. She had been bombarded with phone calls expressing interest. Still, she explained that she was telling everyone who called that she was waiting to hear from "the nice young couple with two sweet girls."

I took that as a sign that we were destined to live in the old farmhouse. By summer, we were the proud owners.

It was wonderful to have a home of our own, but there was much work to be done to get the house in order. The largest bedroom was in the worst shape, so cleaning and repairing it was the first order of business. On breaks, my husband read the newspapers that were under the faded rug. He said he felt like he was in a time warp as he read the front-page reports of the Vietnam War.

Beneath the newspapers, he found an oak floor. Directly in front of the closet, someone had cut a square in the floor and replaced it with new wood. We wondered why it had been replaced, and what might be hidden beneath the floorboards, but the mystery was just one of many out-of-the-ordinary things we found as we excavated our new house. Before long we'd forgotten about the strange square, our attention drawn to a box of old books that had been left behind. Inside the box, we found an autograph book sporting dates from the 1800s. In our kitchen, we found a book that was used to record remembrances from meals eaten at the house. The date on the book was also in the 1800s. As we cleaned out cabinets, we rescued items that seemed to tell stories. There was also a box of dinner napkins with a price tag of fifteen cents still attached. Yet, what was hidden below the wooden square upstairs remained a mystery. Lively thoughts on why it was there and what might be beneath the square on the floor were commonplace.

One afternoon, my teenage daughter, Angela, asked if I would come up to her room. Always glad to be welcomed into her realm, but somewhat troubled by her serious request, I followed her upstairs. We entered the now bright yellow room covered in whale and dolphin posters. Angela sat down cross-legged in front of her closet and ceremoniously removed the throw rug, exposing the wooden square.

"Mom, can we try to get this up so we can see what's inside?"

Relieved that was all she wanted, I readily agreed. "Let me go down and get my toolbox," I said, but she smiled and pulled out the small toolbox her daddy had given her for Christmas the previous year.

"So, you were expecting a yes?"

She smiled. "I was hoping."

We worked together, trying to remove the nails. The harder it was to open, the more excited we became.

"I've been trying to pry this open ever since we moved in here," she confessed. "I always stopped because I was afraid I might damage the surrounding wood." Her serious look made me giggle and she smiled with relief.

"So, what do you expect to find inside?" I asked.

"I don't know! It's been killing me to sit on my bed and see it. I kept imagining a hidden treasure. Finally, I covered it with this rug so I could sleep at night."

I smiled. "I thought the rug was for decoration."

"Well, that, too . . ."

When the square loosened, I started to lift it off and Angela placed her hand over mine.

"Mom, what do you think is inside?"

"Your hidden treasure!" I kidded.

We were like two kids preparing to open a treasure trunk. Together, we lifted the wooden square off and looked below. We immediately burst out laughing. Our treasure was the electrical workings for the porch light that hung below. After we stopped laughing, Angela looked at me seriously.

"Mom, I'm sorry. I've kind of made a mess. Do you think we'll be able to get it back right?"

"Honey, it's not a problem," I assured her. "Now we know how to get to the porch light if needed."

Together, we put the wooden square back in place and hammered it down the best we could. We laughed and smiled at the adventure we had undertaken. Angela thought we hadn't found a treasure, but I smile every time I think about it, for we did indeed find a treasure—the greatest treasure, a memory that was far better than any other item we had uncovered in our old farmhouse.

Clinging to the Past

by Laverne Bardy-Pollak | *Union, New Jersey*

I PULLED THE LADDER DOWN from the ceiling and climbed the shaky rungs into my attic. It had been many years since I'd entered that dark space, but an exceptionally heavy April storm had me concerned over a possible leak.

Upon reaching the top of the ladder, I pulled the overhead string that hung from the ceiling and the sixty-watt bulb shed light on a number of cartons I had no memory of. I was puzzled. Surely I was the one who had placed them there, but when and why?

I peeled open the tape that neatly sealed the first box, peeked inside, and instantly recalled how they had ended up in my attic.

When I moved into my small home eleven years ago, I knew I had limited storage space, so rather than get rid of my cherished memorabilia—as my children had strongly suggested—I'd filled these cartons, hauled them to the attic, and forgotten about them.

As I sat crossed-legged on the dusty, splintered floor emptying each box, I became lost in a time warp. The floor was my canvas, and the assorted articles that encircled me in varied sizes, colors, shapes, and textures were the medium depicting my life.

I found my grandmother's irreplaceable recipes, and as I closed my eyes and clutched them to my chest, I could taste her mouthwatering knishes, kugel, and blintzes. As a youngster in the early fifties, I followed her around her basement kitchen, noting each ingredient she used to magically create her delicacies. As she skillfully tossed spices and herbs into the simmering kettles on the stove, I tried to figure out the measuring equivalent for handfuls and pinches.

How could I give up my dear late brother's matchbooks and hotel keys collected from his many trips around the world, his journals filled with stories of presidents and beggars he'd befriended, and his poetry that gave insight into his soul? Could I part with his pillow that I press to my face in search of his familiar scent, or his Rolodex, tightly crammed with his lifetime of relationships?

And what about my father's collection of first-edition post-cards? He had been a letter carrier in our small town back in the early 1940s, and had proudly displayed the shiny number 1 on his cap like a badge of honor. I recalled his stories about mail deliveries made on foot in snowstorms, and the friendly homeowners who greeted him with coffee and hot chocolate. His ready smile, charisma, and compassion had made him a legend in the small farming town of Union, New Jersey. Could I hand his prized postcards to a collector for mere monetary reward?

Could I throw away my mother's treadle sewing machine that had been passed down from her mother? She made all of our clothes with it. One year my brother and I proudly presented her with a modern Singer with a zillion attachments. She was embarrassed that she couldn't get the hang of it and continued using her old machine—in secret.

My mother was a beautiful, elegant woman who delighted in dressing up. She had countless pairs of gloves in supple leather, decorative lace, and soft cotton, in every length and color. Could I sell them to a stranger at a garage sale, whose interest would be only in the attached price tag she would press to have lowered?

How could I throw away my children's primitive drawings and handcrafted creations, given to me with love and pride so long ago?

My home has never been simply a place to eat and sleep. It is my sanctuary. It reflects and encompasses my life. Nearly every surface is covered with tangible evidence of my family's existence in the form of photographs, porcelain and crystal animal collections, pottery, ceramic dolls, collages, and paintings. My past and my present coexist.

I've always derived great pleasure from living in the moment, but I find equal merit in preserving yesterday.

I accept the fact that I am too emotionally involved to objectively sort through those boxes with a goal of getting rid of things. It will be a job best left for my children when I'm gone. I hope that in their pursuit of neatness and organization they don't miss out on experiencing the wonderful surge of emotions that come with sifting through one's history. Hopefully they will be fortified with memories and disclosures, just as I was when I found myself sitting on the attic floor surrounded by pieces of my past, in yet another failed attempt at throwing away what my home doesn't need, but my insatiable spirit covets. ౼

The Jewelry Box

by Linda Kaullen Perkins | *Sedalia, Missouri*

I HAD BEEN IN THE ANTIQUES MALL about ten minutes before I discovered the jewelry box. My fingers dented the padded blue top as I picked it up. With a few quick twists of the windup key, notes of "Dance, Ballerina, Dance" tinkled sweetly. It reminded me of a summer day back in 1955.

One long, hot afternoon, with nothing else to do, I stretched across my bed watching the two little neighbor kids, Jeanne and Jimmy. I could only hear bits of their conversation, so after a while my thoughts drifted to the beginning of summer vacation, before life had become so boring. One of the most exciting things to happen had started the second week we were out of school.

"Listen," Mama had said, as she clamped a clothespin over a sock.

"What?" I stopped in the middle of the clothesline I was wiping off.

Mama shaded her eyes and looked toward the street where the sound of melodious notes filled the air. "I can't believe I'm seeing one of those in Sedalia, Missouri." She shook her head. "Look over on the next block."

On Boonville Street, I spotted the music box on wheels. The white jeep, with a red-and-white-fringed top, offered door-to-door ice cream. From that day on, the sound of ice-cream music sent kids flocking into the streets, clutching dimes, waiting for a cold treat.

That summer day, as the voices of the neighbor kids drifted in through my bedroom window, an idea came to me. I jumped up from the bed, grabbing my blue jewelry box from the dresser. The key clicked as I gave it several turns. If my plan worked, this day might not be so boring after all.

I looked across the street to make sure Jimmy and Jeanne were still playing outside. They were still chatting to one another, as innocent as the day was long. I stifled a giggle and placed the jewelry box against the window ledge and the black window screen. Bars of "Dance, Ballerina, Dance" floated through the air. Then, as quick as I could, I yelled at the top of my lungs. "Mama, can I have a dime for the ice-cream man?"

"No," she called from the back porch where she was absorbed in painting the floor. "There's ice cream in the freezer."

Just as I had hoped, Jimmy and Jeanne jumped up and raced toward their front door. "Mom," they called, "can we . . ." I smiled and stifled another giggle. My plan was working. In a few minutes, they returned, their hands clenched tightly into fists.

"Is he on Boonville?" Jeanne asked as she glanced down the street.

"I'm not sure," Jimmy answered.

I clapped my hands over my mouth, snorting. This was better than I had expected.

"Let's go down to the corner," Jeanne shouted.

I grabbed the jewelry box, rewinding it before racing to the next open bedroom window.

"Listen, he's getting closer," Jimmy squealed.

I started laughing and couldn't stop, rolling on the bed, cackling.

"What's the matter with you?" Mama asked as she walked into the bedroom.

"Those kids!" I wiped the tears from my eyes and pointed. "Look at them running up and down the street. They think the ice-cream man is coming." Mama looked from me to the music box and her mouth dropped open.

Aiming a gray-covered paintbrush at me, she declared, "You ought to be ashamed of yourself! You go right out there and tell them the truth."

Mom was serious. I immediately got up off the bed and headed to the front porch.

"Hey, Jeanne and Jimmy," I called, choking back one last giggle. "What are you two doing?"

Jeanne's sky-blue eyes sought mine, a wide smile exposing two missing teeth. "Look," she said, opening her hand, "we have ice-cream money today."

"I don't see him anywhere," Jimmy said as he ran up to us, sweat trickling down his face.

Looking at his anxious eyes, I swallowed hard. "Well, uh . . ." My little practical joke didn't seem funny anymore. "There is no ice-cream man."

That was all Jeanne needed. In seconds, she'd burst into tears.

Jimmy patted her on the shoulder. "Don't cry," he whispered. Looking up at me he asked, "Where did he go?"

I felt my face grow warm. "Well, you must have heard my jewelry box," I said, searching for words. "You see, it plays music." Wanting to escape the disappointment on their tearstained faces, I turned away. "I can go get it." Just then Mama came out of the house.

"Here, kids." She smiled as she handed Jeanne and Jimmy each a double-decker chocolate ice-cream cone.

As she turned and started back inside, I looked at her in bewilderment. "Mama? Where's my cone?"

Without so much as a backward glance, she snapped, "Get it from the ice-cream man!"

A Ride on Grandma's Glider

by Linda C. Wisniewski | *Amsterdam, New York*

SOMETIMES A WEEKEND AWAY FROM HOME can become a trip back in time. Last summer, when my husband and I arrived at our bed-and-breakfast, I was pleasantly surprised to see a 1940s porch glider, much like the one my grandmother had owned. In an instant, my mind traveled back to the 1950s, to my beloved grandmother's front porch.

In my memories of Amsterdam, New York, my cousin Wayne remains a little untamed. He and Aunt Geneva came in on the Sunday afternoon train and arrived at Grandma's wrapped in a whiff of danger. They walked alone from the train station and climbed the hill where Grandma lived, while my sister, Judy, and I waited on the porch.

My sister and I were good little girls who knew how to behave. We sat on Grandma's glider, a white metal contraption with green plastic cushions and loose pillows printed with huge gray flowers. It squeaked with the slightest movement. We were careful to push off gently, toes to the floor, rocking slowly with just a tiny squeak on the backstroke, but when Wayne arrived, things got kicked up a notch.

"Hi Linda! Hi Judy!" *Plop!* Wayne's bottom bounced onto the seat. In a heartbeat, he pushed off the floor with both feet, the glider squeaking like a rusty gate. Wind whistled past our ears. We rocked forward and back so fast there was no time to touch the floor with our shoes, no time to help push, no time to slow down. Wayne was in total control, and we loved it. We shrieked and giggled and the glider squeaked and the grown-ups heard.

Grandma came running out in her corduroy house slippers, and Mom and Aunt Geneva told us to stop it right now. Of course, we did, but Wayne couldn't resist temptation for long. Always, a few minutes later, he'd start again. Pushing, pushing, faster and faster with his feet, until his bottom lifted off the sticky plastic and came down with a squish on every forward glide. We heard an awful scraping sound as metal hit the wall, and then running footsteps.

"Way-nee! That's enough!" Aunt Geneva marched onto the porch and grabbed him by the ear. "We're going home right now!"

"I'm sorry, Ma! I'm sorry!" Wayne knew he'd gone too far. "I wanna stay, Ma. Can we stay long, Ma?"

"If I catch you doing that again . . ." His mother frowned and went back to the kitchen.

"Let's play inside," I suggested. Wayne agreed, and immediately dumped a bag of green plastic soldiers onto Grandma's coffee table and arranged them into battle scenes. Then he showed us his latest war comics. For Judy and me, Wayne was the perfect Sunday playmate. He brought us a kind of danger where no one got hurt. Even when he turned Grandma's hassock on its side, rolled it across the floor and tried to jump on, and overshot, landing on his head, he escaped without a scratch. We heard another chorus of "Way-nee! We're going home" followed by "I'm sorry, Ma . . ." Wayne pushed the envelope and got yelled at, but he didn't let that stop him from having a good time. No instigators we—Judy and I were happy to go along for the ride.

We got older and stopped riding the glider. Wayne joined the army after high school, went to Vietnam, and earned three Purple Hearts. When he came home, for a moment I saw his old bravado.

"They ought to send 'em all to Vietnam!" he said, laughing at an antiwar protest on TV.

I was a college student, against the war. I didn't know what to say. I loved my cousin, but he wasn't playing soldiers anymore. This was real. Our eyes met, and his grin collapsed. In a flash, I wished we could all go back in time and sit on a white metal glider and play with green plastic soldiers.

"Nobody should go there," he said, looking at the floor. No longer an untamed little boy, Wayne—like all of us—had changed.

I moved away after college. My job and adult life became all-important, and I didn't go back for Wayne's wedding. I would today, though. These are my people, their memory the spot I pushed off from, the wind whistling past my ears.

Return to Irish Town

by Annette H. Sharp | *"Irish Town" Montpelier, Louisiana*

I WAS UNPACKING WHAT SEEMED TO BE an endless supply of boxes from my move when I ran across a single key on a green, heart-shaped key holder. It was the key to Grandpa Dan's property that now belonged to my mother, Joan. The old house still stands. The square-headed nails, heart of pine pillars, and quilting hooks in the twelve-foot living-room ceiling attest to the age of the home. The cedar trees marking the lane that leads to the house now blend into the surroundings. Years ago, those trees marked a bittersweet journey my grandmother never forgot, a story she'd shared with me so many times I could see it as if it were just yesterday. . . .

❧

The Model-A chugged its way up the hill and across the last three miles of the trip. Dirt roads and rain made the ruts a little deeper in rural Louisiana, and there seemed to be more rain this June than there had been in the last few years.

◄○►

146

I spotted the row of cedar trees. Grandpa's house was but a minute away. Octave honked the horn twice and the familiar *ahooga* sounded out to announce our arrival. Joan, a six-year-old bundle of energy, hardly sat still. She was so excited about the trip that she barely slept the night before and was already up when Octave and I awoke at 4 A.M.

Joan had quickly dressed herself in the cotton dress that I had made for her the week before, and then combed her hair. She shifted from one foot to the other as I insisted on combing her bangs out of her eyes and securing her hair with a barrette. All the bags were carefully placed in the car along with a large lunch and some cookies and pies that were for sharing with Grandpa.

The trip was very exciting for Joan, who could not remember very much about her Grandpa Dan. She wanted to know more about the world I had shared with him, a world that lived inside my heart but had never been allowed out or shared with my only child. To find out what she could, Joan occupied several hours of the trip by asking questions.

"Why is it called Irish Town?" Joan quizzed.

I glanced at Joan's sweet, innocent face and wondered how much I should tell her about the hardships of growing up. "Well," I said, "Grandpa Dan is Irish."

"Did they name an entire town after him?"

"No sweetheart, there are many Irish families who settled around the same area where Grandpa Dan lives." It was easier to explain that you lived in the back woods of St. Helena Parish if you said that you lived in Irish Town. The locals all knew which roads and which families were a part of Irish Town. The answers seemed sufficient—at least for the next five minutes or so—then the questions started again.

"Why doesn't Grandpa have a wife?"

"My mother, your grandmother, died of yellow fever many years ago."

"How did she get yellow fever?"

Again, I wondered how much of my life I should share with Joan: the sorrows, the loneliness, the orphanage, the death of a sister and a brother. Hesitantly, I picked through the details and shared those I felt she was ready to hear. She was so young, she didn't need to know how hard life could really be.

"You get yellow fever from mosquitoes," I said, but quickly added, "that's why we spray for mosquitoes at home and that is one of the reasons why Grandpa moved away from New Orleans."

"Oh," was all Joan had to say. She didn't appear concerned about mosquitoes or yellow fever. Her questions were directed at learning more about her grandfather. Without skipping a beat, she shot another barrage of questions at me.

"Why was Grandpa in New Orleans?"

Another tough question. There were no easy answers. Certainly none a six-year-old would understand, but I did my best. I tried to share with my only child what America meant to so many immigrants who were fleeing Ireland—first to survive hunger, and next to survive by making some kind of a living. Many prominent Irish people were largely penniless and had to work as laborers. But along the river there were slaughterhouses, tallow factories, steam-driven cotton presses, and even a sugar refinery. Work could easily be found. It took decades of hard work and savings to be able to move into the less-crowded surroundings.

"Grandpa Dan arrived in New Orleans, where he met my mother and married her. He found work in New Orleans, so they lived there, and my siblings and I were all born there," I said.

"What's a sibling?"

"It means brothers and sisters."

I guess my silence about my family for so many years warranted the inquisition today. Tears started welling up in my eyes and I turned my head toward the side window as if I were peering out.

I still remember all the hush-hush whispers the evening my mother died. I was the oldest, then Emma, Stephen, and Mary. They had all gone to bed but I couldn't go to sleep because somehow I knew that I was about to lose my mother. She had been very, very sick. My father's face, drawn and suddenly aged, showed the toll of both my mother's illness and then of her death.

The question I didn't want to answer, Joan asked next. "Where are your sisters and your brother?"

I stared straight ahead. "We all went to stay in an orphanage."

The Catholic nuns took us in and cared for us. We didn't get to see Dad much after that. It was in the orphanage that Emma got sick and died, and there, too, that my brother, Stephen, took his own life. But this was not something I wanted my child to know. When Joan started to ask another question, I changed the subject.

"It's time for lunch," I said as cheerfully as I could. "Let's pull over and eat."

After lunch, Joan was finally exhausted enough from lack of sleep from the night before and the bumping along for seventy-or-so miles in the old Model-A, that she fell asleep in the back. When she awoke, much to my grateful relief, she had forgotten her previous line of questioning. We ate up the remaining miles by talking about what we saw along the countryside and what Grandpa Dan was doing now.

Then Joan startled me by asking a real grown-up question: "What are you looking forward to the most, Mom?"

I turned away from my daughter as memories crowded in and the real threat of a deluge of tears dominated my emotions. I needed my father's hug and his acceptance that I was still his daughter no matter what had happened growing up. I needed his laugh, his violin playing, or "fiddling," as he called it, on the porch after dinner.

"I just need to see him, sweetheart," I said quietly. "I just need to see him." ✑

Reels of Love

by Sande Boritz Berger | *Merrick, Long Island, New York*

THERE WAS A FEELING OF PURE JOY whenever Dad announced he would be showing our home movies. While waiting for the first huge silver reel, my brothers and I began the ritual of creating shadow bunnies—our fingers diving, colliding, and bending against the stark white wall.

Vintage cartoons preceded the films: they were always black and white, starring an anorexic Mickey Mouse. Like the films, the cartoons were silent, but the darkened room where we sat shoulder to shoulder roared with our laughter and commentary. No one "shushed" anyone. There wasn't any dialogue to miss—just the cranking of that old 16mm projector, which echoed through our modest split-level home, a home situated in a small town called Merrick, which is eight miles from the Atlantic Ocean on the south shore of Long Island.

For me, an awkward adolescent, the home movies affirmed that I was loved. In the scratchy, faded images, I saw my face cupped and kissed by my grandmother, the family matriarch and loyal best friend. At a birthday, Mom and I, hands clasped, led "ring around the rosy" with plump little cousins wearing ridiculous party hats.

The camera nose-dived when Dad apparently ran after me as I tried to maneuver a shaky two-wheeler down a too-narrow driveway. We poked each other, embarrassed by any shot of our parents smooching. Dad slim in Navy whites, Mom's Rita Hayworth hair swept back in a snood. Had he deliberately set up the camera to record this for posterity? Hungrily, we absorbed reel after reel, anticipating the flapping sound, our signal to whine for another. There was the face that seemed to freeze-frame the action, halt our laughter—a favorite aunt who had died suddenly. Years later, I learned she had taken her own life. Watching her braid my hair in these films, I relived the sadness of losing her—thought I heard the hushed voices at the time of her death.

Then, when I was in high school, Dad began traveling. There was less time for family recreation and fewer home movies taken. It felt as if we were all being catapulted into the future, and I wondered if we would get another chance to look back and reflect on what we stood for or who we were.

After I married, my parents and brothers moved to Florida. Feeling no close ties, my husband and I also moved, to Boston, and for the first time the family was really scattered. When I became pregnant, before buying a single book on prenatal care, I raced to a camera store to purchase a Super 8mm movie camera and projector. I was fanatical about recording the pregnancy on film, as well as friends' visits, casual dinners, and poker games in our crowded walk-up.

I was dedicated to my new role as historian, filming my own children's parties, dance recitals, vacations starring parrots and dolphins. I edited animated stills at each film's opening, but I was aware of how my movies seemed so staged. They were much too modern, these "talkies." They lacked the richness of pure motion and the magical charm reflected in the smoky silent films of my childhood.

Then one day my father pulled the old reels from storage. He'd seen an ad for transferring them to video, dubbed music included.

Not long afterward, my brothers and I each received a cassette. It was labeled, "Home Movies . . . Our Children." It had been decades since we watched these movies together, and now we each viewed them separately, 1,500 miles apart, in our own homes with our own families.

The video opens with Paul Anka singing "The Times of Our Lives," and I break down before the first frames. I'm startled by a familiar image of me at three trying to blow out the birthday candles on a fluffy pink cake. My lips curl and quiver until some help appears behind my shoulder. To my surprise the candles go out, and I beam a gummy smile toward the camera. I watch these movies alone wrapped in an old crocheted blanket. My heart pounds and I'm afraid to blink—it's like seeing things for the first time. There's a strange mix of loss and reacquaintance. My grandmother, her hair in a perfect chignon, looks cautious and worried as she walks beside me. The aunt whose death forever haunts me flinches from the camera lens. She is self-conscious and unsure. My parents embrace in a passionate kiss. When did I ever see them kiss like this? I'd already forgotten. I find myself talking aloud to the faces, until the video abruptly fades to black, and I sit staring at a blank screen.

I call my Dad to thank him. "Yes, the video store did a great job." He tells me the cartoons were too old to transfer.

"Save them Daddy," I say.

A decade passes. My oldest daughter is getting married in forty-eight hours. Although she and her fiancé live together, she announces that, following tradition, she will spend the night before her wedding in our home, sleeping in her old bed. She warns us she wants a quiet evening, no guests or stress. For hours, I rack my brain over how to spend this special night. And then the idea comes to me, like a forgotten lyric. I call my youngest daughter from the car and ask her to gather the shopping bags containing our Super 8 films. We rush to a local camera shop. Yes, they do transfers. Of course, I'll pay double for the overnight service.

After an early dinner, I blindfold the bride-to-be and her sister guides her to the den, practically pushes her into the rocker. We are all giggling when she begins to balk, wedding nerves intruding. I turn on the VCR and Paul Anka croons once more. Removing the blindfold, she sees a four-day-old version of herself—a baby Buddha nuzzled in my arms. I hear her hearty laugh but tears are brimming. Then a small voice says, "Thank you, Mommy."

The gift I give her—these home movies—are the films of *her* childhood, a catalog of *her* young life. If she should ever stray or forget her past, she will have them, as I have mine—the indelible proof of how much she is cherished. ∾

Out to Lunch

by Gloria MacKay | *Cloquet, Minnesota*

LITTLE GIRLS CARRY SHINY PINK PURSES. When my granddaughter walked in with hers, it was not the purse, but the color, that spun me around. Where had I seen precisely that shade of pink before?

What came to mind, instead, was the feel of Aunt Clara's snap-together coin purse clutched in my hand. But it had been black and scruffy, cracked where undyed leather showed through. As I told my granddaughter, it wasn't pretty like hers.

Memories are like kernels of popcorn—when one bursts open, you know you're going to get a whole lot more. It wasn't long before I remembered a certain afternoon in a small Minnesota town, and I even recalled where the pink fit in.

I would have never dared to lunch alone when I was nine years old if it hadn't been for that purse. To this day, women don't like to go out to lunch by themselves. With a partner or friend? Just ask. But when we're alone, we'd rather down a deli sandwich in the car than undertake a solitary sit-down luncheon at a table preset for two.

I was nine years old, all by myself, and hungry. I sat down at a table for two in the best restaurant in town—the only restaurant in town—back in the 1940s. I suspected the waitress wondered if I had any money, but she took my order—the same thing I ate with Aunt Clara—cheeseburger, fries, and a chocolate malted in a cold metal shaker twice as big as the glass.

We usually sat at the counter, but the last empty stool was almost hidden between the girth of two men with elbows sprawled and a newspaper spread between them. I picked the little table by the door.

Lunching out was actually the second big event of my day. I had already walked the few blocks down the tree-cooled street from my grandmother's house to the beauty shop to get a haircut. I had clutched Aunt Clara's little black purse, so bulging with coins it wouldn't fit in the pocket of my shorts, hands sweaty from the heat and the responsibility. Before I had time to worry about losing my way, I stood in the beauty shop doorway, not sure what to do until Gladys motioned for me to sit and look at a magazine. She was topping off a very old lady, hunched under plastic, with blue-white hair as wispy as smoke. Gladys almost lifted the woman off the swivel chair. As soon as her feet struck the ground, like a wind-up bird, the woman darted out the door.

I climbed up, cradling the purse on my lap. Gladys must have talked to somebody because she didn't ask how much to cut. She just snipped away and brushed me off. That was my signal that it was time to pay. As I struggled with the snap, the coin purse popped open and money shot out like big silver BBs. I spent what felt like the rest of my life nose to nose with the shiniest pink floor—the only pink floor—I had ever seen.

I managed to count out the correct amount, remembering an extra quarter just as my grandmother said. I was not sure why, but Gladys must have understood. She didn't try to give it back.

So there I was, on the sidewalk, sun beating straight down on my new haircut, my mouth dry as dirt and my stomach as empty as the purse was full. What did I do? I walked into town and took myself out to lunch. Not uncomfortable, but feeling very serious, I ate my cheeseburger, most of the fries, half of the malted, and then I asked for a cherry cola and slurped it down with a straw. The waitress, smiling now, watched me count out the right amount of change, leaving a little extra, again, like Aunt Clara did. I was fortified for the hot walk back to Grandma's.

When I got back home, lunch was almost over, but nobody asked if I was hungry. I was grateful because I didn't want to eat another lunch or go into detail about where I'd been. However, I was a bit puzzled. When Grandma set out food everyone ate, but this time, no one questioned when I passed up a meal. Though I hadn't thought that much into it at the time, I now understand a small town is a hard place to keep a secret.

These days, I stop for a bite at the mall or drag in a bag from a drive-up window, but I have never again lunched alone. I have this recurring dream where the maitre d' asks, "How many are you expecting in your party today, ma'am?" I say something flip like *zero, zilch, zip,* or *nada.* Folks around me look up. I smile. They look down at their plates. My waiter feigns concern. "Would you rather order or wait for the rest of your party?" I order. I eat. He says, "I'll be your cashier when you're ready." Then he stands there, waiting.

"I want a little dessert," I muse. I eat every crumb.

"I will be your cashier when you're ready," he repeats. He stands there.

"I would like a touch of Drambuie, please." I sip.

The busboy tries to clear my table, but I slap his hands as I gulp a cherry cola. Finally, I pull out Aunt Clara's little cracked black leather snap-together coin purse, toss a handful of small change on the white tablecloth, and sashay away.

I'm tired of dreaming. I've already read "How to Dine Alone" tips, which dictate you should nestle with a newspaper, make lists, fantasize about the people sitting around you, if you will, but most of all enjoy your own company.

If this works for dining, why not lunch? I'll bring my battery-operated, hand-held bridge game. If I get too flustered at my fantasies I could retreat to the powder room and regroup. I doubt there will be anyone stationed there to inquire whether I want to use the facilities now or wait for the rest of my party!

I'll manage, just as I did when I was nine, although you can't buy lunch with small change anymore. I don't know what happened to Aunt Clara's little black leather coin purse, anyway. It's funny the way it got tangled up in my mind with that shiny pink floor, the exact color of my granddaughter's purse. But isn't that the way with memories? As soon as you take off the lid, they bounce around like popcorn. ❧

Cloquet, Minnesota

Destruction and Restoration

*I*n 1879, following the Civil War, Cloquet was in need of wood to rebuild the town's war-ravaged homes. Cloquet built its first sawmill on the St. Louis River at Knife Falls. From this site, "Wood City" grew and prospered.

On October 12, 1918, a forest fire completely destroyed the settlement of Cloquet, Moose Lake, and many additional small towns in the area, taking more than 450 lives. Nearly all the homes and buildings were destroyed. According to one eyewitness, the railroad depot agent, Mr. Fauley, contacted other railway agents, asking them to send as many railcars as possible. His quick thinking saved many Cloquet residents. Since then, history in Carlton County is dated as "before the fire" and "after the fire." Following the devastation, residents put their shoulders to the task and rebuilt Cloquet from the ground up. ✍

How the Town Was Named

*T*hough there is no documented proof regarding how Cloquet got its name, residents have clung to several possibilities. One suggestion is that the name is derived from the French word *claquet*, which refers to the sound of the mill, and another suggestion is that the name Cloquet is a derivative of the French name Cloutier. According to some residents, a man by the name of Cloutier was traveling by boat on the nearby river and became stuck. It is thought that the river was named after him and sometime later the settlement was named after the river. ✍

Town Facts

First incorporated • Cloquet was incorporated in 1884.

Location • Cloquet is located in the heart of the north woods, on the St. Louis River, about thirty minutes south of Duluth on Highway 135, and approximately two hours north of the Twin Cities.

Industry • In the 1880s, Cloquet was one of the largest logging and lumbering centers in the world. In addition to lumber, the mills produce paper, wood pulp, and matches.

Places of note • Several Cloquet landmarks are on the National Register of Historic Places, including the only gas station built by famous architect Frank Lloyd Wright, the log Indian Church of SS. Joseph and Mary, the Northeastern Hotel, the Park Place Historic District, the Old City Hall Building, and the Shaw Memorial Library, which now houses the Carlton County Historical Society.

Interesting people • Democratic presidential candidate John Kerry visited Cloquet in 2004 during its Centennial Celebration; in 1922, the Minnesota Democratic Party nominated Anna Dickie Olesen of Cloquet, who became the first woman endorsed by a major political party to run for the Senate. Movie actress Jessica Lange was born in Clouqet in 1949.

Cloquet is very proud of its hockey program and the people who have been involved in it. Jamie Langenbrunner and Corey Millen, two noteworthy hockey players from the 1999 Stanley Cup Champion Team the Dallas Stars, played hockey for Cloquet High School.

Interesting facts • Cloquet can trace its roots back to the seventeenth century and the arrival of French explorers.

Sisters of Summer

by Roberta Beach Jacobson | *Lake in the Hills, Illinois*

CHILDHOOD MEMORIES came flooding back the day I found the dilapidated old beach ball, long forgotten in the back of my closet. What I remembered most was that, like other children, I had imaginary playmates, but mine were always sisters.

Overall, I had few complaints about being an only child, but when my junior high school sponsored a Sisters Spaghetti Gala one Thursday evening, I felt left out in the cold. The next day in school all the girls swapped stories about who ate (or spilled) the most spaghetti sauce and which sister said what. I felt like the only girl in the world without a sister.

Sure, I had friends. But having a sister—someone to share clothes, records, and secrets with—was my number one goal. Besides friends, I had a dog and plenty of toys, records, and books for entertainment, but having no sister, I tried to explain to my parents, left a huge void in my life. I longed for a sister of my own. Just as important, I wanted to be a sister.

In the summer of 1968, revolution and change were in the air. Pammy and her family were summer people. She was stuck with three brothers, and her days were usually spent hearing about or playing flag football, softball, and volleyball. What she longed for was a sister, someone to share girl secrets with.

"I can't tell my stupid brothers if I think a guy is cute," Pammy complained to me, with all the wisdom of a fifteen-year-old. I understood her dilemma perfectly. Having a sister meant there would always be someone there to listen. If only we'd had sisters, we both dreamed, our lives would be complete.

By the July Fourth fireworks, I'd exchanged my prized red Nehru jacket for Pammy's granny glasses and elephant bell-bottoms. It was a wonderful, sisterly feeling! It was a joyful summer for us, one when we were way too old to play with dolls but far too shy to flirt with the boys at the beach. Our biggest worries that summer were what shade of lipstick to buy and if our bodies would ever be womanly enough to fill out a bikini.

Before hitting the beach, she and I spent hours in my bedroom listening to Beatles albums and styling our hair, and every day we swam under the summer sun. Living on a lake meant all activities involved water or the beach, which we loved. Besides, Lake in the Hills, Illinois, didn't offer much else to do. It had no stores—not even a post office. But kids learn to make their own fun, and Pammy and I got by that summer on our imagination.

Pammy's birthday, in mid-August, always signaled the end of our summer fun together. We both knew that, in a couple of weeks, she and her family would pack up their car and head back to the city heat, and I wouldn't see her until the following summer.

That year, Pammy was turning sixteen. Although her "dumb brothers" were oblivious to the fact, Sweet Sixteen is a major event in a girl's life. It is a reminder that womanhood is fast approaching. I realized the occasion required a special gift and a heartfelt greeting card.

After endless shopping, I selected a John Lennon–style corduroy cap. I knew Pammy would appreciate it. I also knew her card had to be unique. I scanned card racks in store after store before I spotted *the one.* The card was delicate and lacy, covered with pink roses.

Best of all, it read, HAPPY BIRTHDAY TO MY SISTER.

Sisters—that was it! Just like sisters, Pammy and I had done everything together that entire summer. We'd shared our clothes and had private discussions regarding which boys we thought were cute. In our hearts, we really were sisters. The card made it official, and from that point on, we both knew we were not alone. ⌒

Single Shot .22

by Carbon Rains | *Calvin, Oklahoma*

I WAS CHECKING OUT A STEREO SYSTEM in one of the local pawn-shops when a young woman came in carrying a .22 rifle. She asked the clerk how much he could lend her on the firearm. The balding man with the beer belly took the gun from its case and barely glanced at it before the words came out of his mouth.

"I can lend only two dollars on it." The lady's gasp was heard clear across the shop. Perhaps feeling somewhat guilty, the clerk added, "Look, it's only a Single Shot .22. They aren't worth anything."

I almost said aloud, "Boy, are you wrong!"

In my home, a Single Shot .22 stands ready for use at any given moment. My feelings about it are, in part, based on sentiment, since I inherited it from my father, but also due to the fact that that little Winchester is what kept my father's family from going without during a hard spell that lasted several years.

It all started in 1921, with my grandfather, Albert Ringgold, and a red mule. That mule was a handsome beast, but mean as any varmint that breathed. He bit people as well as the farm animals. On one cold January morning, Red made the mistake of ripping a chunk of flesh out of Grandpa's shoulder. Grandpa immediately tied the errant mule to the back end of a wagon and drove to Calvin, Oklahoma, which at the time was a busy farming community, on Old 270, southeast of Holdenville.

Along about midmorning, Albert and Red arrived in town. People noticed the good-looking mule and began to ask about him. Everyone said such a large, handsome animal would be perfect for pulling the family wagon, an excellent addition to their team. Grandpa worried that Red might bite or kick one of the interested farmers, but Red was on his best behavior that day and sold within the hour. Albert Ringgold took the proceeds from the sale and stopped off at the gunsmith.

The next day, on my dad's birthday, Grandpa handed his son a Winchester .22. That winter, Dad supplemented the family meals with squirrel, rabbit, opossum, and raccoon. It wasn't just the meat that he put on the dinner table, which often was the only meat on the table, but he also sold the pelts and purchased bolts of material, which Grandma needed to make their clothes. Later, in his teens and young adulthood, Dad often took off Saturday from the fields so he could take his nieces and nephews to the movies in Holdenville, using money he'd made from the sale of the skins.

At a family gathering a few years back, my cousin told me that these Saturdays were some of her fondest memories of childhood. Not just the movies, which were the same for a whole month, but also getting to spend the entire day with Uncle Fred.

In my lifetime, I also remember how important a Single Shot .22 could be. In 1958, Oklahoma suffered one of the longest droughts in its history. That fall and winter, Dad kept food on the table with the Winchester. I still recall one cold morning when he took me to the woods with him. We brought home almost a dozen rabbits and even more squirrels. We survived off the land that winter and all the next year on wild game, all bagged with that Single Shot .22.

When Dad died of cancer in 1985, my brother, Bill, and I divided his belongings. Among the items I took was the .22 Winchester. I really didn't think it would be used again for hunting, at least not in my lifetime, but I wasn't ready to part with it.

In the fall of 1989, my friend Laura asked if I would take her and her son hunting.

"He wants to go hunting so badly," she explained, adding that neither her husband nor her son were hunters, and that her uncle, who lived in Kansas, wouldn't take the boy hunting until he'd had some experience under his belt. She further implored, saying he had a rifle and could hit the target.

I wanted to say no. My idea of hunting these days is finding the best cut of meat at the local butcher shop. Instead, I said I'd think about it and called my uncle, Van. He was very excited at the prospect of taking a novice hunter out on the farm, and we made plans to take the boy and his mother hunting the very next Saturday.

Unfortunately, we got a late start. By the time we arrived at Uncle Van's house, the dance was over. It's a known fact that if a hunter isn't in the fields by 6:00 A.M., the game will go home. Squirrels and rabbits have no tolerance for latecomers.

So, rather than hunt live game, I decided to do some target practice. After getting the targets all set up, I told the young man to go ahead and shoot.

Jason looked at me with dark brown eyes and quietly confided that he had never shot a gun.

After a few quick lessons on proper handling of a firearm, we did some serious target practice and the Single Shot .22 did not disappoint any of us.

In 1921, that Single Shot .22 gave an eight-year-old boy much pleasure and self-esteem. It enabled the boy to contribute to his family's dinner table. It also gave him the means to feed his own family during lean times. Sixty-eight years later, it gave another boy, of approximately the same age, the necessary experience he needed to join grown men on a pheasant hunt in rural Kansas.

I don't know what memories the woman's Single Shot .22 held for her or her family, but if her gasp was any indication, there were many. And as I thought about it, I realized there was no way my Single Shot .22 would ever see the inside of a pawnshop. ᢙ

A Sign of Love

by Lorna M. Kaine | *Elkins, West Virginia*

THERE WERE ALL SORTS OF RELICS in my mother's house, but the one I regarded as special was a copy of the Hagerstown Almanac that I found after Mom's death. Seeing it reminded me of how much the almanac affected our lives when I was growing up in the small town of Elkins, West Virginia.

In 1945, spring didn't pay any attention to the calendar. March came in like a lion and growled its way into a cold, wet April. Crocuses pushed their way through snow to bloom, but most other flowers waited for warmer weather. Throughout May of that year, my grandfather made a fire in the potbellied stove in the dining room. Even so, seeds he had ordered from the seed catalog began to arrive in the mail, and Granddad managed to spade his vegetable garden during the few warm days we had. Our country was still fighting World War II, and most everybody in town thought it their patriotic duty to plant a victory garden. But Granddad would have planted his garden, war or not. He had a lot of mouths to feed since my mother, sister, and I had moved in after my father's death. Besides, Granddad had been a farmer most of his life and enjoyed growing things.

Granddad always planted his garden by the sun and moon signs given in the *Hagerstown Almanac*, in his mind the only almanac worth having. Sweetpeas were my grandma's favorite flower, and Granddad always planted them for her on her birthday as a special gift.

March 17, 1945, arrived with howling winds, sleet, and temperatures in the thirties. As I left for school in the morning, I saw Granddad looking askance at the sky. When I returned that afternoon, he was out by the fence planting something. I didn't stop to ask what he was planting—it was freezing out! When I got in the house, I found Grandma in the kitchen making bread.

"What's Granddad putting in the garden?" I asked.

A smile lifted the corners of her mouth as she shook flour through her sifter. "Sweetpeas," she replied.

Granddad was sopping wet when he came in, but I noticed he was smiling, too. After he'd had a chance to dry off, I asked again what he'd been planting.

"Sweetpeas," he said. I was puzzled. Granddad wasn't one to plant flowers before the vegetable garden was completely in. Besides, it was freezing cold out there.

"Why?" I inquired.

"Because today's the day the almanac says to plant peas." Granddad then picked up his newspaper to let me know I shouldn't ask any more questions.

"Oh, you planted the garden peas, too," I said matter-of-factly.

He shook his head. "No," he replied, "just the sweetpeas."

I frowned, trying to understand. "Shouldn't you have planted the garden peas, too?"

Granddad lowered his paper. "Yes, but it was too cold to stay out there and do it."

Wide-eyed, I asked, "Will the garden peas grow if you plant them another day?" I had already absorbed the importance of doing things by the almanac, and I was worried what would happen to the pea crop if Granddad deviated from its instruction. I got the feeling I'd stretched his patience thin when he straightened his paper with a snap and spoke from behind it.

"Probably not as well as if I'd planted them today, but we'll have a crop."

That June, when the sweetpeas formed a crazy quilt of reds, pinks, lavenders, and whites against the fence, Granddad picked the first flowers and took a bunch to Grandma. She stopped her work long enough to bury her nose in the bouquet's fragrance, and once again I saw her smile that certain smile that she reserved for special moments.

One of my jobs was to arrange flowers into a centerpiece for the dining-room table, so I asked, "Do you want me to put them in water?"

Grandma shook her head. "I'll take care of these," she said.

After the war was over, and my grandparents had long since passed away, my mother still kept to the tradition of planting by the *Hagerstown Almanac.* Sometime during my teenage years, I asked her to explain the signs to me. I am ashamed to say I never really learned any of them except the moon phase ones. The one thing I did remember, though, is that March 17 is the day to plant sweetpeas—no matter if Mother Nature dumps sleet or rain or thirty-degree weather onto the earth that day. I call it the "sign of love day" because Granddad's love for Grandma prompted him to plant her favorite flowers that day in spite of inclement weather, and the smile on her face told me she felt that love and returned it. ❧

The Ice Ball Machine

by Guy Carrozzo | *McKeesport, Pennsylvania*

WHEN MY TWO CHILDREN WERE YOUNG, our family took a vacation from California to McKeesport, Pennsylvania. It was a nostalgic trip. I was showing my kids where I had lived when I was a little boy.

While walking down a particular street, I noticed an old one-car garage that brought back some instant memories. It was showing years of neglect, and if it weren't for the adjacent brick building propping it up, it probably would have collapsed years ago.

As I peered through the small windows in the garage door, it was difficult to see anything because of the accumulation of spider webs and dirt. But I was determined to see if a very important part of my childhood was still locked inside this dilapidated structure. I wiped the window with my hand and peered inside again. And there it was . . . broken down and almost unrecognizable. It was what we kids back then called "the Ice Ball Machine." I quickly lifted my son and daughter up so they could take a peek. They were not impressed . . . but I was . . . *wow!* As I gazed at that machine, my mind drifted back in time to another era. In 1943, an eleven-year-old boy and his pals had to be creative to pass the time during summer vacation.

◄○►

I lived in a small town outside of Pittsburgh—a town of steel mills, railroad tracks, a slaughterhouse, junkyards, and coal barges that plied the rivers delivering coal to the mills. Money was in short supply and our immigrant parents had never heard of the concept of giving their children an allowance.

The high point of our day was when we heard the shout of the Ice Ball Man as he made his way through our town. I can still hear his melodic chant, "Ice Ball—Ice Ball—get your Ice Ball today!"

An "Ice Ball" was the prototype of the snow cone of today. The Ice Ball Man pushed a two-wheeled enclosed cart with sliding glass windows and a twenty-five- to fifty-pound block of ice inside. He used a tool that looked like a wood plane to shave off thin layers of ice that he then scooped up with a large ice-cream scoop and put into a cone-shaped paper cup. Then came the sweet part: the different flavors that he squirted onto the ice from bottles that were lined up in a row—strawberry, orange, cherry, lemon, and grape—were out-of-this-world delicious!

The price of an Ice Ball with one flavor was two cents, and a penny more for each additional flavor, or all five flavors for a nickel. We usually got the one-squirt kind and we were grateful for that. That was sixty-one years ago, and as I write this story, I can almost taste the flavors again. On a miserably hot, humid August day, sitting in the shade and sucking on a cherry-flavored Ice Ball was as good as it got—or so we thought until we discovered the giant Ice Ball Machine.

On one of those hot muggy days, my friends and I went down to the river to cool off. It was on our way home that we passed the icehouse at the top of a slope that went up from the river. We went up to see if we could get a chunk of ice so as to cool off. As we approached the building from the back, we had to go through some heavy foliage. There was wooden lattice framework around the base of the icehouse, I guess to help with ventilation. As inquisitive boys, we pulled the strips of wood partially off so we could enter the basement. Once we were inside, we realized the air was quite cold. As we quietly walked around the basement, our eyes slowly got accustomed to the darkness . . . and suddenly there it was. To us it was a sight to see—breathtaking, shocking, mysterious—a six-foot-high mound of snow. Naturally, we wondered how it got there. Then we figured it out.

We were under a giant saw that sawed the 500-pound blocks into smaller and smaller blocks weighing anywhere from 25 to 100 pounds so they would fit into various-size iceboxes. The ice mound was a by-product of the sawing of ice, like sawdust is a by-product of sawing wood.

Was this not the greatest treasure that a group of kids could find on a hot summer day?

Soon we were burying ourselves in the snow, eating it, piling it high on our heads—throwing snowballs at each other in August.

The smallest kid in the group compared our situation to sitting on or in a giant Ice Ball. We all couldn't have agreed more, and it would have been exactly the same, if only we had had a few bottles of orange and cherry and grape flavoring. As we were enjoying ourselves, we heard the motors of the saw start up and then the shrill screeching as the blade of the saw started to cut into the ice block. Ice particles began falling on us as if it were snowing. The snow dusted our faces as it continued to replace our wonderful ice ball with fresh layers of snow. Could it get any better?

We returned often to our special "Ice Ball House" that summer. It was a summer none of us will ever forget. ❧

Penny Memories

by Cheryl Pierson | *Calera, Oklahoma*

AT THE BOTTOM OF MY OLD JEWELRY BOX lies a treasure that I had once forgotten for over thirty years. The two pennies, flattened by the roaring, sparking wheels of the MK&T Flyer that made its daily run through the sleepy little southeastern Oklahoma town of Calera, have dulled in the passage of time, but they will always be special to me.

My cousin, Julie, and I were ten years old that summer and restless for adventure. Whenever we were able to steal away from our grandmother for some alone time, we headed down the narrow two-lane road that split the town, leading to the train tracks.

The hot summer days were the best. Julie and I would raid our mothers' coin purses for change—Mercury-head dimes, nickels, and pennies. We'd begin our long walk, our colored rubber thongs slapping against the hot concrete.

The midway mark to our destination was a small store constructed of cinder blocks with a concrete floor. Petey's Grocery was a wonderful place. The wooden screen door opened with a twangy screech as we entered the dim interior. A rattling box fan and a water cooler, draped with a thin wet towel, provided the only relief on those hot July days.

There were short rows of sparsely stocked canned items, and on a high shelf near the top, around the sides of the small store, were a few hurricane lanterns and metal washtubs. In the glass case near the front door was red-rind bologna and cheddar cheese that Petey sliced and wrapped for his customers to carry home for lunch. But what Julie and I wanted was in the case in the middle of the store.

The red-and-white Coca-Cola case was nearly chest-high. We'd slide the metal top to the side, then plunge one hand into the freezing cold water, pulling out a soda pop as chunks of ice floated past our numbed wrists. Petey kept that case well stocked with bottles of orange and grape Nehi, Coca-Cola, and Dr. Pepper.

We paid our nickel and took that first sweet drink, letting the cold liquid slide down our dry throats, knowing nothing had ever tasted better. Nothing, except the Baby Ruth candy bar we bought to go with that cold liquid fire, which we now sipped in an attempt to make it last longer.

We set out once more for the tracks to wait for the two o'clock train. Once we stepped onto those metal rails, we reveled in the feeling that we were truly alone, having escaped from the houseful of younger cousins. No one knew where we were, and we never spoke of it. Carefully, we laid our pennies on the ribbon of metal, then moved away a few feet to walk on the railroad ties and share our innermost secrets.

After all these years, I can't recall the particulars of those talks. Details, like the two copper pennies I have rediscovered, have dulled with the passage of time. The feeling of anticipation consumed us as we waited for the long row of snaking, grinding metal cars. Had we missed it? Did it run on Sunday? As two o'clock drew nearer, conversation lulled between us. If we talked, we might not hear the rumble of the wheels.

"Is that it?" Julie would ask, gripping my arm in excitement.

I'd listen hard, then whisper, "No. Not yet."

We felt the vibration before we ever heard anything. Then, far away, the thunder of the rolling wheels became faintly audible and the shiny glass eye of the light swung into view, staring at us accusingly. Our hearts beat like hummingbirds' wings in excitement—and, maybe, a little fear.

We moved away gradually, and suddenly, it seemed as if we couldn't get back far enough, quick enough! The roar was deafening, conversation impossible. From several yards away, we'd wave at the engineer, who always blew extra blasts on the whistle just for us, and we'd stand, silent, in awe, until the caboose went by, so we could wave at the brakeman. To us, they were heroes, those railroad men. We waved until the caboose disappeared. At last, we'd run to get our flattened pennies.

Walking back slowly, we'd drop off our empty soda bottles at Petey's for a penny deposit, satisfied with our day. We'd had our time together, sharing the excitement of the train, the proof clutched in our brown hands. Those flat pennies were an unbearable secret that no one could know about. Although we both longed to go back to Granny's and make the younger cousins envious, we didn't dare. We never wanted to give our parents an inkling of where we'd been. Next time, it might be forbidden.

Sometimes when the long wail of the midnight flyer pierced the night, I'd awake in the protective summer shroud of darkness, thinking of our earlier adventure, at peace, feeling like I'd come home from a long, long journey. Believing that the dreams two young girls shared really could happen—someday.

The Big Dipper had, by then, swung around in the velvet palm of the night sky, so that I could look right out the latched screen door and see it from my pallet on the floor. I'd close my eyes, imagining that I raised my hand in salute as the grinning brakeman waved me back to sleep, and the hum of the metal box fan became one with the sparking click of the wheels on the track.

Those two pennies mean even more to me now than they did then, during those childhood days of summer. As I hold them in my hand, it's as if I can taste the first clear, cold swallow of Petey's soda. I feel the heat of the July day rising from the concrete road Julie and I walked together, and I am reminded of my youth, and of trains, and dreams that will never be again, all in a flattened piece of copper.

The Times They Aren't A-Changin'

by Leslie A. Friesen | *Dallas, Oregon*

A FEW TREASURES, like small towns and old friends, remain motionless in time amidst the whirlwind of change that envelops a lifetime. For years, my path has crossed that of the same group of men around our small town of Dallas, Oregon. I remember the younger version of these guys sharing coffee in a long-closed diner. In the prime of life, these busy husbands and fathers served in church, coached soccer, and led community clubs.

It was a favorite joke among the six to tease the youngest—and baldest—of the buddies.

"Guess I'd better go get a haircut today," said the balding one, sipping black coffee.

The others soberly sipped their own black coffee and nodded in agreement. Inevitably, someone replied, "Yep, better go get those ears lowered," and the men erupted into laughter. Fists pounded the table and cups clanked against chipped saucers as they howled at the cornball humor.

Last week, I purchased a mocha decaf at my favorite coffee shop, across from the stone courthouse. A table in the corner displayed a collection of antique coffee pots and china cups and saucers. I gingerly examined a delicate rosebud-patterned cup and was drawn back in time to the days when coffee was served in china instead of paper latté cups. Nearby, three men now sat alone at their usual table with their usual drinks at their usual time. Where had life taken the missing three?

Thick silver hair crowns the tall man drinking coffee white with cream and sugar. Retirement suits him well. His tan face is aged, but not mapped with lines.

Only a thin rim of slate-gray hair trims the nape of the second man's neck. His weathered face and hands bear the marks of life spent farming in the Oregon rain and sun. I know he hasn't retired because farmers never retire.

The final, and completely bald, man is the class clown of the senior set. He recycles the same corny stories year after year, and year after year, the men laugh. After thirty years, they no longer laugh at the punch lines but rather at the absurdity of continuing to tell the same stories. At the silliness of their own ritual. At the oddness of growing old together.

As I paid for my mocha, the bald man announced that he'd best go get a haircut today. I smiled as I walked out of the coffee shop. I knew what was coming next.

"Yep. Better go get those ears lowered."

There were no peals of laughter this time, only knowing smiles and twinkling eyes. ∾

The Laugh Took the Prize

by Lynn Ruth Miller | *Toledo, Ohio*

I OPENED MY GRADE-SCHOOL SCRAPBOOK and there it was: the award I had won in the seventh grade in speech class. The ivory-colored parchment had a blue ribbon attached to the right-hand corner, which read,

FIRST PRIZE
LYNN RUTH MILLER
7TH GRADE SPEECH COMPETITION
JUNE 2, 1945

I still remember how proud I was to win that award. I was a quiet child who enjoyed writing and dreaming. Public speaking terrified me almost as much as the woman who was supposed to instruct me in the art of elocution.

Her name was Helen Fox. She was my homeroom teacher. She also taught history and speech. She was stereotypical of the old-maid schoolmarm: strict, uncompromising, and often cruel in her criticism of the children she instructed. She prided herself on her inflexible discipline. "A rule is a rule," she would say. "That's the way it is in life and the way it will be in this classroom."

She believed that, because those rules were the boundaries that hemmed in her life. She was not an attractive woman, nor did she try to be. She wore the same tailored skirt and red jacket every day in the classroom and also when she taught at my Sunday school. She pulled her obviously dyed black hair into a severe bun at the nape of her neck and wore sensible lace-up oxfords. She was plagued with allergies. When she wasn't pronouncing historical sequences for us to memorize, she was sneezing, coughing, and blowing her nose with explosive vigor.

Susan Godfrey, the principal of Fulton School, was also a spinster, but one who enjoyed the freedom of a single woman even in the early 1940s. Her posture was so erect she looked as if a yardstick were glued to her back, but none of us doubted how much she cared about us. On one occasion, when Miss Fox sent me to the office for whispering, I was forced to sit on the naughty bench with a cluster of children who threw spitballs and fought with each other at recess. Miss Godfrey emerged from her office and beckoned me to her room. I followed her, tears of shame streaming down my face. She walked over to me and took my hands in hers.

"Lynn Ruth," she said. "Throughout your life, you will meet people so wrapped up in their own pain that they don't recognize the special gifts of those around them. You will often be falsely punished, and just as often, you will follow all the rules and fail in the result because your judge doesn't want you to succeed. When this happens, my dear, you must force yourself to feel compassion for the person who seems to be your enemy."

She paused for a moment and handed me a tissue. "Now dry your eyes and go back to your classroom."

Miss Fox taught Speech on Friday afternoons. I lived in agony that I would say something wrong and she would chastise me in front of the entire class. It seemed like Monday through Thursday vanished like the wind and I was faced with the torture of knowing I must perform for a woman who didn't like me, moments after I had survived my last poor performance. However, after Miss Godfrey's little talk, I began to look for things about my teacher that made her human. Miss Godfrey had hinted that my relationship with this stern woman was soured by something inside Miss Fox and I tried to figure out what that problem was.

As I trudged home that afternoon, trying to find a suitable topic for my speech, I thought about all the idiosyncrasies that set Helen Fox apart from the other teachers. There was her dress, of course, and her inability to smile. There were her allergies and her sense that no one ever understood what she was trying to teach. There was her unbending posture and the way she paced in front of the room like an expectant father. As I thought about these characteristics, I had a great idea. I would incorporate all of her idiosyncrasies into my speech the next day and call it "How Not to Give a Speech."

I stood in front of the class the next day, my hair pulled back into a bun, wearing a red jacket, a navy blue skirt, and very large lace-up oxfords. I held a Kleenex box in my hand, cleared my throat several times, and began to cough and sneeze. I paced up and down before the class as I announced, "A rule is a rule. That's the way it is in life and the way it will be in this classroom."

Then I blew my nose. I frowned at my giggling classmates and said, "When you laugh and whisper you are not learning. You are wasting my time!"

I shook my finger at the class and sneezed so violently the papers on my podium scattered across the floor. I looked at Miss Fox, expecting to be sent down to Miss Godfrey again, and relaxed. She was laughing!

Miss Fox put her arm around my shoulder and actually smiled. "A sense of humor is the only weapon you will ever need in life, Lynn

Ruth," she said. "I have never been able to abide people who take themselves too seriously."

At the end of that year, Miss Fox presented awards to her students and I won first prize. I was shocked . . . and very proud. I learned an important lesson that day. I realized that no one will remain an enemy once you share a good laugh. ∽

Strong Stuff

by Barbara Brady | *Oketo, Kansas*

I was a city girl from suburban Chicago until 1955, when I married a minister and moved to Kansas. We were assigned to Marysville, Kansas, population 3,800, plus a few cats and dogs. In addition to the church my husband served in Marysville, he was also assigned a small church in Oketo. It wasn't long before the immediate culture shock shifted to an appreciation for small-town living.

We drove ten miles on a muddy gravel road, past cornfields and pastures, to find the town of Oketo. Marysville was a metropolis by comparison. Oketo had an unpaved main street, a post office, a limited grocery store, and our church. A good imagination was needed to believe the reported population of eighty. On a good Sunday, church attendance was about eighteen, but later increased to thirty.

The church was a white frame building with a small spire, much like one in a Norman Rockwell painting. The chancel had an altar, pulpit, and piano. The church had all the necessities—everything, that is, but a bathroom.

What the church lacked in luxuries, though, the congregation made up for with their warmth and cordiality. Warda Argo, longtime member, unlocked the church on Sunday mornings, turned on the heat in winter, and opened windows in the summer. She also served as church pianist and often provided our family with homemade goodies. She exemplified the expression "pillar of the church."

My husband served the Oketo church for a mere two years, but it was long enough for me to gain a new appreciation for small-town solidarity. When we left, I missed the authenticity and small-town camaraderie, and, in particular, Warda Argo, who demonstrated commitment and strength.

We moved several times and lost contact with Oketo friends. More than forty years passed before we returned to Oketo, on a nostalgic journey into the past.

"I wonder if Warda Argo is still alive," I said, not really believing in the possibility. But when we located her house, I couldn't believe my eyes when she came to door. Like us, she had aged and she walked slowly, but she greeted us with her usual warmth.

"I don't move as fast now," she said as she plopped into her comfy chair. "A stroke a few years back put a crick in my left side, but I get around pretty good."

We recalled how she knew every hymn in the book and would begin playing the first hymn when she heard our car pull up in front of the church. Her face brightened. "Oh, yes, I remember," she said. "I am still playing. We have a small organ now."

"What! You are still playing!" I thought my ears were playing tricks.

"Yes. I have played for seventy-six years," she replied.

With some coaxing, she shared her story. "I started lessons when I was six years old. I had a good teacher," she said, obviously wanting to give credit for her talent to someone else. "We didn't have many people around here who could play the piano. I started playing for the church service when I was ten years old." She paused and smiled. "And I've been playing ever since."

I glanced around her modest home. "Do you get paid?" I asked.

She scoffed. "Of course not. I never got paid. I just do it."

She grinned. "Some preachers like to spring new hymns on me. I fool them. I play them all."

"Do you ever miss a Sunday?" I asked.

"Sometimes. When the weather is really bad after a snowstorm, church services are called off."

"I guess you'd be there no matter what the weather," I commented.

"You bet!" she answered.

Sunday morning, at 9:30 A.M., Warda Argo wouldn't be anywhere else but at her church, sitting on the piano bench—unless it was at the organ.

They don't make people like that anymore.

Oketo, Kansas

Population: 90

First Settlers

A plaque on the side of an old stone building at one corner of town is just one of the many reminders of Oketo's enterprising early settlers. The sign reads, Z.H. MOORE GENERAL STORE, FIRST STONE BUILDING, 1884. Ziba Hibbard Moore, whose name is on the plaque, was born in 1845 in Pennsylvania. In 1875, he moved to Gage County, Nebraska, and obtained work at the nearby Indian reservation. In 1879, he moved to Oketo and established a store and then later a bank. He and his wife, both birthright Quakers, were not swayed from their purpose when they discovered there was not a Friends church in Oketo. Instead, they began attending the Methodist church, while at the same time fulfilling Ziba's wish to educate the local Native Americans, which he and his wife did until the Native Americans moved on to Oklahoma.

The building functioned later as a post office, until 1970. It was placed on the National Register of Historic Places in 1976. In 1972, it was turned into a museum known as Oketo Community Museum, which is open by appointment from April to November. The museum is a testament to the people of Oketo, who value remembrances of the bygone era of 1875–1899. ❦

Town Facts

First incorporated • Oketo was incorporated in 1870.

Location • Oketo is located in Marshall County, in Oketo Township, on the Big Blue River, approximately ten miles north of Marysville, which is the county seat. In the early days, Oketo had many stone quarries. Existing stone buildings include the former jail, bank, two stores, and the opera house. Today most of the buildings are used for storage.

Interesting facts • In 1889, Kansas became the first state to include prohibition of alcohol in its constitution, leaving Oketo dry until 1986, when the legislature passed liquor "by the drink," depending on the county. This situation was remedied when Nebraska, with no such legislature, and being just three miles away, was eager to offer up liquor for a price.

Place of note • The name Oketo (pronounced oh-key-toe) derived from a famous Otoe Indian chief named Arkaketa. Numerous Otoe artifacts have been collected and are on display in the Oketo Community Museum, including a few of the chief's personal items. In addition, the museum is pleased to have in its possession a contemporary painting of Arkaketa, painted by one of his great-grandsons.

Transportation • From 1850 through the early twentieth century, as many as 200,000 children were transferred by train from overcrowded orphanages and homes in the northeastern cities of the United States to live with families on farms throughout the Midwest, via the Orphan Train movement.

Oketo was on the main line of the Overland Stage route and served as a main trading point. The Pony Express also operated one mile outside of town. Today, a stone barn and corral denote the site of the Oketo Stage Station and Trading Post, built in 1848.

Almost Heaven

by Joyce A. Anthony | *Titusville, Pennsylvania*

TUCKED AWAY FOR TWENTY YEARS in a dark corner of the basement, the box, alone and forgotten, was easy to miss. When I spotted it, I pulled it into the light, intending to toss it with the garbage, but curiosity worked on me and I had to open it.

I found the harmonica buried beneath the death notices and funeral books. I turned the cold metal over and over in my hands, noticing how the shine had been dulled by the years. I raised it to my lips and found the sound still sweet and clear, and memories came flooding up from my very soul. Whole scenes played out before me, and I was a child of seven again.

Spending a week with Gramma was always special. Her house overlooked a large yard that sloped downward. Grass wasn't something you found often in the city, and I loved the feel of it beneath my bare feet. Fall was my favorite time because the air smelled of ripe apples and the grass was tall enough to form an outdoor carpet, perfect for rolling down the hill over and over again until the whole world was spinning. The bottom of the hill straightened out enough so I stopped rolling before I reached the train tracks that passed by.

I don't think I ever thought about being in danger. The tracks were somehow friendly, at least to my young and trusting mind.

Just as the sky became a mixture of pink, orange, and blue, the long, low whistle from far off in the distance summoned me to run back, halfway up the slope, to wait. The ground vibrated gently, as if the grass were humming because it was happy. Then the train appeared. It chugged past slowly, never seeming to be in a hurry to get anywhere. I waved and the engineer never once failed to smile and wave back, giving one short pull on the train whistle as if to say farewell until tomorrow.

Just about that time, Gramma would call me back to the porch for a cup of fresh apple cider that the neighbors had sent over. I loved the way the sweet-tart taste made my tongue tingle as the cider passed over it. When Gramma reached into her dress pocket, I settled down happily. I knew what was coming. Gramma held that harmonica as though it was the most precious of treasures.

When she blew that first note, the sound echoed throughout the darkening evening. All became still, as though nature itself were waiting in anticipation. A moment later, the clear, lively notes of "Big Rock Candy Mountain" filled the air. Gramma always started with this one because it was my favorite. My feet twitched as the notes danced around me, enticing me to join in.

As the evening wore on, the music turned to the old gospel tunes Gramma had grown up with. She'd sing awhile, her voice as high and clear as the music she played. Gramma closed her eyes and poured her heart out, louder with each hymn, and every so often, she paused to tell me a story she remembered about growing up in the mountains. She made the stories sound so real, it didn't feel as if she was talking about strangers. It was as if I had been right there with her, milking goats, churning butter, and running in the fields. Each song seemed to take her deeper into her memories.

Running her fingers over the surface of the harmonica, she spoke of her dad. Her voice would become soft as she talked of how he loved to play music. When Gramma told me how her mother gathered all twelve children together in the evenings, her face glowed with the love she felt for her mother, still. The family gathered and read from the Bible, then her daddy, my great-grandfather, would start playing his harmonica and my great-grandmother would sing. All those years later, Gramma still believed her mother had "the voice of an angel" when she sang. I knew it couldn't have been more beautiful than Gramma's singing voice.

Night would have fallen by then and we'd head back inside. Gramma would tuck me into bed, still singing softly. I'd drift off peacefully to the sounds of "Amazing Grace" mingling with the scent of ripe apples and a picture of the mountains. All was right with the world.

It is amazing to me, even now, how a three-inch-long instrument made in Germany in the 1890s always gave me a glimpse into what heaven must surely be like—the air alive with harmonica music and the high, sweet voice of an angel come home.

Sunshine

by David E. Morton | *Caldwell, Idaho*

IN 1976, TWENTY-FIVE YEARS after having moved away, I had an opportunity to visit my hometown of Caldwell, Idaho, where I had grown up in the 1940s and '50s.

Caldwell was more than a Main-Street-and-one-stop-sign kind of town. It had a few traffic lights, and even boasted three movie theaters. But it was small enough that most everyone knew everyone else. For example, when I was watching a Saturday matinee at the Fox Theater at the ripe old age of six, an usher quietly padded down the aisle with his flashlight and said to me, "David, your dad is here to pick you up." How he knew my name or where to find me, I don't know. But it didn't seem odd to me at the time.

Now, as I drove through town in my rental car, I viewed the street names, which had always seemed to be "standard names," chiseled in stone. There was Fillmore, Dearborn, Cleveland, Maple, and Walnut—didn't all the towns and cities of the world use these names? And there was my first school, Lincoln Elementary School, on Grant Street, where Miss Bates taught first grade. Miss Bates even brought some books and assignments to our house when I was sick with the measles.

We lived on Ash Street, across the street from a small liberal arts college called the College of Idaho. The C of I was as cozy and friendly as the town—laid back and easygoing. The nice thing about being a little kid during that era was that you could go almost anywhere and no one would stop you. I would wander into Sterry Hall, the gymnasium where they once held a game of Donkey Basketball with real donkeys, and into the biology department, where I was received with a friendly greeting. Many of the students and professors even knew my name.

My dad, the music professor, worked in a small two-story building called Blatchley Hall. Blatchley Hall was an attractive building with white columns fronting its Grecian entrance. Seeing it again brought back memories of a tough day in the life of a five-year-old kid: the day my dad left for work without kissing me goodbye.

It was around 1948, and I had just finished eating breakfast while watching the rain splatter against the kitchen window. After a while, I realized that Dad didn't seem to be around, and asked Mom where he was. She replied that he had gone to work.

What? How could he do that? He hadn't kissed me goodbye!

I marched to the front closet, donned my raincoat, and headed out the front door before my mom knew I was gone. I trudged along through the rain, past the tennis courts, across the campus—crying all the way—until I finally arrived at Blatchley Hall.

As I climbed the front steps, I heard singing coming from the second floor. I pulled open the front door and began ascending the steps to the second floor, where my dad's office was located. The voices grew louder with each step. They were singing "You Are My Sunshine."

I turned the knob to the classroom door, opened it halfway, and slipped inside. There were about thirty college students warming up their voices, my dad directing from the front of the room. I stood there for a moment, dripping wet, red-eyed, and desperate. As if on cue, the students noticed the drenched little elf standing in the doorway and the singing stopped, and I knew that this was my moment.

"Daddy! You forgot to kiss me goodbye!" I said in a clear-as-a-bell voice.

My comment earned uproarious laughter from the students, and I'll admit that even I chuckled a little when they laughed. Dad motioned to me to come up to the front of the classroom, which I did, shedding tears and rainwater every step of the way. When I reached his side, Dad enveloped me in his arms and kissed me.

In that instant, my world was right again.

That kind of informal, friendly access is what I remember most about growing up in a small town. When I was seven, I drove the college tractor for a few days, helping to cut sod. I got rides on the town's road graders—with my mom's permission—and rode around town while we graded the outlying gravel roads. A steam locomotive engineer offered to give me a short tour of the switching yards riding in the cab, but I was too scared. To this day, I kick myself for not taking that opportunity. Occasionally, a yellow Piper Cub would fly over the house, so low that I would wave to the pilot—and he would wave back.

And whenever I see a picture of a drenched little kid in a raincoat, I think back to that day when I burst into my dad's classroom and pleaded my "Sunshine" case. Small towns, and the safety and innocence of the era, made that kind of childhood possible, and those memories still have the ability to breathe a little sunshine back into my life. ∾

Putting Down Roots

by Marcia E. Brown | *Pike County, Illinois*

"INDIAN TERRITORY!" The very name frightened my grandmother, Emma, when my grandfather, Will Jacobs, proposed they move to Muskogee. To pull up roots from her home in Pike County, Illinois, and travel to a community she had heard of only as the newly established capital of the Five Civilized Tribes—that scared her.

But "*Go West, young man*" was the rallying cry of the twentieth century, and Will heard it loud and clear.

"It was 1901. Our children were only sixteen months and two months old when your granddad decided there was a better future for us in the West," Grandma explained.

As farm children from large, close-knit families, neither Emma nor Will had ventured far in their young lives. Pop-Pop, as I called grandfather, had the rare advantage of a college education and had gone on to graduate from the Louisville College of Dentistry in Kentucky. Dentistry was a brand-new science, not accepted by everyone. When most folks had a "bad" tooth, a barber wielding pliers took care of it for them.

Although she was a homebody and a little shy, Emma soon caught Will's spirit of adventure. When he made the decision to move to an area that would not achieve statehood as Oklahoma for six more years, Emma accepted his decision. She was still frightened, as she envisioned a dangerous place filled with hostile people in a wild land.

"In those days, though, wives went where their husbands decided," she said. "And Will chose a new life in a new town for us."

"But Grandma," I asked, "wasn't it terribly hard to leave your mother, your brothers and sisters, your friends, and everything familiar?"

"Yes, it was! I cried and cried when we got on the train in St. Louis, and the babies cried, too. But I had something special with me that made it all much easier after we arrived."

"What was that?"

"I'll show you, honey," she said as she led me to the mahogany sideboard in her dining room. From a drawer crammed with keepsakes as diverse as knitting needles, from when she'd stitched woolen socks for World War I soldiers, to a pair of my baby shoes, she pulled out a small, battered brown envelope.

"This is one of the little packets that held garden seeds given to me when your grandfather and I left home to come to Muskogee," she said.

Peering closely at the envelope, I could see faint penciled lines that read, "Four-o'clocks."

"This held seeds from my mother's garden for my own first garden. My married sisters and my cousins all gave me little packages of seeds, too. My brothers gave us seed corn and melon seeds from their farms. My best friends gave me cuttings from their roses."

Grandma's face glowed as she remembered.

"You know that pink rose bush your Mama has from a start of mine, the one that's covered with hundreds of tiny blooms in June?

That is from a cutting I brought with me way back then. The four-o'clocks around our back steps today are descendants of those that grew in my own mother's yard all those years ago.

"It was just the right time for planting when we finally got to Muskogee," Grandma continued. "Those first weeks, I was almost too scared to go outdoors alone, but Will had found a house for us with an extra lot. He was busy setting up his first dental office but he got a man to dig a garden. And by midsummer, we had flowers and plants from home taking hold. Just like us, they were putting down their roots.

"So when I looked out my windows or sat on the porch with our babies, I was surrounded by a love garden. When I smelled those first flowers, I felt like I was being hugged by folks who loved me. And you know, my first friend there was a Native American neighbor who loved flowers, too. She and I traded plants and talked about our gardens, and soon I realized I was putting down some new roots myself."

Over the years, I often heard my grandmother say, "A lot grows in gardens besides flowers and vegetables. There's also friendship and fortitude, but most of all, love." ∾

Moving On

by Carol Nyman | *Felton, California*

A HURRIED MOVE FROM THE CITY to the cabin in Felton, California, had created havoc. At the cabin, there was no attic or garage for storing things, so the unfinished "garden room" became the unofficial attic. Over the years, the old boxes were pushed farther to the back, newer interests taking premium space.

Years later, a decision was made to go through the boxes and eliminate the unnecessary stuff. It was a big job, but I was slowly making progress toward one corner. As I lifted one box, I spied a square black suitcase that I recognized instantly. Without even opening it, memories of the year I turned thirteen came flooding back.

That was the year I was given my first bra. I remember it so clearly. My mother measured and determined the correct size I would need to "train" my development. The package I had long awaited was laid on my bed that afternoon.

Later in the evening, when no one was around, I tried on the white cotton garment. There was a problem—a big problem—but I was too embarrassed to mention it to my mother. I looked in the mirror, pulling at the extra fabric. The bra was very pointed. My developing womanhood was not—hence the extra fabric. After much deliberation, I came up with an idea. I grabbed some fabric scraps from my mother's sewing box and stuffed the points. It took me a while to get the balance correct, but at last I found the perfect stuffing.

The next step was to try on several sweaters. I was impressed. I showed more than I really had, and a vision of Betty Grable came to mind. Not her legs, her profile pose that showed she had survived the development stages.

The rest of the evening was uneventful. That is, until I unhooked the bra and the stuffing fell into a pile on the floor. The perfect balance was no longer perfect. I *almost* cried. But in the end, I didn't. I wasn't about to let this woman thing get the best of me. No, siree!

I stomped into the bathroom and grabbed the box of cotton balls. I figured I could count the number of balls I put into one side, then do the same for the other. In no time at all I had used the whole box. I was pretty proud of myself for solving a very ample space problem. Well, until the next morning. When my mother wanted to know where the cotton balls were, I had to relinquish my supply and ended up going to school without my new bra and my newfound Betty Gable profile.

Now that I had been exposed to the possibilities of womanhood, I was extremely self-conscious. I felt like everyone was looking at my developing breasts. I remember being miserable and hoping that the memory would fade over the years. It hasn't. Not because I didn't try to forget, but because my father made a decision that almost ruined my life.

Dad often helped people who didn't have cash fix their cars. They, in turn, paid him with bartered items. On several occasions, he made excellent trades. We ended up with an antique pump organ; a deer head over the fireplace; a deer rug in front of the fireplace; fresh quail, pheasant, and deer meat. The list goes on. This time, however, he came home with an accordion. You could tell by the look on his face that he felt this was one of his best bartering deals. He was so proud that he talked about it all through dinner. We listened to him expound the merits of learning to play this unusual instrument.

I half listened. I was still trying to figure out the bra. I had found that Kleenex, if folded carefully, could temporarily fill the points. I tried on sweaters and blouses and was pleased with the results. Maybe I didn't look exactly like Betty Grable, but I felt I could compete.

I donned the bra the next day and headed off to school wearing one of my favorite sweaters. My figure had improved overnight. By third period, I realized I had problems. The wad of tissue and cotton balls had slipped to the sides. My perfect breasts were now pointing east. I raised my hand to be excused. I was thinking I could sneak off to the restroom and make an adjustment without anyone knowing.

When I got to the restroom, I realized there was only one wad of stuffing. I cringed and hoped no one would notice. One good breast was better than none, I thought to myself. But, in case someone should notice, I stopped on the way back to class and grabbed my coat from my locker. I opened the door to class and looked down. There, for everyone to see, was the wad of stuffing staring back at me . . . daring me to pick it up. I stepped over it and took my seat.

Ultimately, I made the decision to wear the bra without filling the points. This resulted in a crinkling effect under my sweaters, so I added my coat as part of my attire each day.

My father continued to describe the merits of the accordion at the dinner table. I pretended not to listen and made every effort not to join in the discussion. Because he was so excited about this music-in-a-box, I thought he meant he was interested in learning to play, but I kept my head down, not making eye contact, just in case.

I had just made it through another day at school with the crinkled bra and was beginning to feel more confident when my mother commented—at the dinner table—about the ripples under my sweater. I blushed. I just wanted to fade away. All eyes were now focused on my breasts. The very thing I had been trying to avoid at school was happening in my own home. A discussion ensued about the merits of the new bras over corsets. At this point I was ready for the old-fashioned corset.

In passing, my mother suggested that perhaps I should try stitching across the front of the bra and eliminate the pointed area. That's what she had done, she proudly shared with me. I couldn't believe that she would discuss this personal matter in front of my father and younger sister, who sat with a smug grin on her face. I wanted to crawl under the table. I was mortified.

I guess my father decided the conversation needed a new direction because out of the blue, he suggested that I be the one, the only one, to take accordion lessons. I couldn't believe my ears. There I was, struggling to come to grips with the new bra and the unwanted points, and he wanted me to learn how to play a squeezebox! A squeezebox that opened and closed over my breast area? A box that drew attention to the area I tried to hide every day! What was he thinking?

Today, tears kept me from seeing the black box clearly. I reached down, unlatched the lock, and opened the lid. There on top was the sheet music of the last song I had tried to play. The accordion lessons had been dismal, my skills nonexistent.

Later, as I put away the accordion, I realized that opening the suitcase was a harsh reminder that not every second of my childhood had been wonderful, but I also learned a valuable lesson. Memories are what make us who we are and should be replayed often. ❧

The Brass Bell

by Betty Downs | *Clyde, North Dakota*

AS MY MOTHER APPROACHED the final days of her life, I went home to be with her. Seeing the brass bell on the table beside Mother's bed brought tears to my eyes. I had forgotten about the bell, but upon seeing it, pictures of a frightened little seven-year-old girl came to mind.

In 1930, due to the drought, Dad's effort at farming failed, and our family moved into Granddad and Grandmother's big farmhouse located just three miles from the little town of Clyde, North Dakota. The old, unused, narrow hallway became my bedroom. I had my own dresser and a little table beside the single bed, and was extremely happy to have my own space.

The hallway was long and narrow with doors on each end. The bed was in front of the south door, a door we never opened. The north door opened into the big square living room. To the east were two large windows that looked out onto the neighbors' fields and had curtains that blew in gently whenever a breeze wandered by. A long, narrow oak board, with hooks sticking out of it, was on the west wall. In bygone days, it held coats. When it was my bedroom, the hooks served as a handy place to hang my pajamas and blouses. Above me was the railed porch with the tin floor. I loved the convenient hooks for my clothes. I loved the pretty curtains that matched the red-and-white-checkered bedspread that lay across the fluffy down mattress. It was so lovely . . . until that first rainstorm.

Waking, in the middle of the night, to the most horrendous noise I had ever heard took my breath away. The big windows were illuminated with sudden flashes of lightning that lit up the tiny room. The clothes hanging above me were caught by the sudden gusts of wind and transformed into ghostly shapes, creating strange galloping shadows on the wall. The piano in the living room took on proportions of horror as jagged electric streaks danced in the dark night sky. The thunder, loud and terrifying, seemed to be right in the room with me. Rain pounded against the windows and hail screamed against the tin of the porch above me. In my seven-year-old mind, I had awakened in a different world than the one I had gone to sleep in.

I screamed and Mother came running. I cried, I wailed, and clung to my poor mother until the thunder rolled away with a soft murmur and the skies were once again filled with stars.

Mother, in all her wisdom, knew she had to do something. I don't know where she found the bell, but find it she did. Perhaps it was an old cowbell that Granddad had hung around the neck of one of his prize Jersey heifers, or once had a home on one of the leather collars Dad used when he harnessed the team of horses. The old tarnished bell was about two inches tall and square, with a hole in the little handle at the top. That bell rested on the table beside my bed all the years that the hallway was my bedroom. At the first rumble of a rainstorm, I rang the bell and Mother padded softly into my room to reassure me that morning would come and I mustn't be afraid.

The chime of the bell turned my fears into a comforting experience. It wasn't long before I was no longer afraid of storms. I became wonderfully aware of the majestic beauty of a middle-of-the-night,

North Dakota–summer thunderstorm. I became friends with the roar of the invisible rolling thunder. The sight of lightning as it ripped open the sky outside my windows was soon nothing to fear.

Now, it was Mother who rang the bell to call me to her bedside. Roles were reversed as I performed the duties that were required to give her comfort in the dark of night. Often, I slipped into bed beside her and we talked until the dark gave way to morning's light. I like to think my presence was as comforting to her as her presence had been to me, so many years before.

The old tarnished brass bell, with the comforting ring, can now be found in my living room. It reminds me that love can take away all fears, and that love given away is love that returns.

The Diploma

by Barbara Brady | *Neponset, Illinois*

MY CURIOSITY WAS STIRRED when a parcel arrived with an out-of-state postmark. When I noticed my sister's return address, I knew what I wanted to be in the box, but I didn't dare to even hope. Following our mother's death a few months earlier, my youngest sister had cleaned Mom's apartment and disposed of her belongings.

My mind brimmed with thoughts of my mother. By her own admission, she considered her life quite ordinary. Her family disagreed. In her quiet, unassuming way, she modeled intelligence, wit, good-heartedness, and a wealth of perseverance.

While writing bits of family history, it became obvious to me that Mom had struggled long and hard to gain an education, meeting one stumbling block after another.

She grew up in Neponset, Illinois, where her father worked as the village blacksmith. In 1922, at age seventeen, she left home to attend Normal State Teachers College near Bloomington, Illinois. That same year, her father died, leaving her mother with three young children still living at home. To help the family, Mom quit college and taught in a nearby country school. She made $105 a month, but scrimped and managed to save enough money to attend Hedding College, in nearby Abingdon, Illinois. After a short time, the school closed, as did many small colleges during the 1920s. By then, Grandmother had moved the family to Galesburg so the children could attend Lombard College. Mom worked in a dairy and taught freshman biology to pay tuition. This school, too, had to close, and merged with Knox College. Student records were transferred to Knox College, and transcripts and records were shuffled around. In the confusion, Mom never received her coveted college diploma.

Mom married, and during the next chapter of her life reared six children. Tirelessly, she bandaged scraped knees, read bedtime stories, canned produce from her garden, cooked, and cleaned. In later years, she helped Dad in his business, became widowed, and battled cancer.

"I should have gotten my college degree," she said wistfully the few times she talked about her past. Though she had diligently pursued an education and had attended college, she had nothing tangible to indicate her achievement.

I daringly wrote to the administration of Knox College and explained the situation. A week later, I received a phone call from the college president.

"Your mother did earn her degree," he said. "We found her transcripts in the university vault. It clearly states she was eligible for graduation. I want to correct the error."

With the help of the president, a special graduation ceremony was planned. An entourage of children and their spouses, grandchildren, and great-grandchildren were present to witness this ninety-four-year-old woman receive her long-awaited college diploma.

Mom, dressed in the appropriate cap and gown, walked hesitantly into the packed alumni room. The crowd thundered its applause. The university president, trustees, and faculty processed in wearing their distinguished robes. We heard a few short speeches and then came the magic moment. The dean of the college said, "Will the second graduating class of 1999 please come forward!"

My short, gray-haired mother stood. A broad smile covered her wrinkled face. She stepped forward. The room quieted and we heard the profound declaration: "Ethel Fields Netherland, we bestow on you the Bachelor of Arts Degree in Biology."

Again, the audience burst into applause—and tears. Seven decades after earning her diploma, Mom finally held it in her hands. The leather-bound parchment may have been long overdue, but the radiance on Mom's face proved it was worth the wait.

I cautiously tore off the wrapping on the unexpected package in my hands. My heart fluttered like a bird in my chest as I removed the last piece of wadded paper from the box. Inside, carefully protected, lay the memento I most desired: Mom's college diploma.

I Wouldn't Have Missed It for the World

by Joan Clayton | *Melrose, New Mexico*

WHO REMEMBERS THOSE World War II defense stamp corsages? Or how about gasoline rationing stamps with the motto "Loose lips sink ships"? Being a child in the quaint little town of Melrose, New Mexico, which had less than 500 people at the time, I took the war effort seriously.

I lived with my grandparents and spent many hours waving to the army-camouflaged truck caravans passing by, and counting the cars pulled by railroad engineers in those big black steam-puffing engines. Back then, everything was rationed, even silk stockings. When someone gave my granny a pair, she thought Christmas had come in July!

Life was not always easy, and certain things, such as the sight of the depot manager walking down the road with a telegram in hand, had the power to put fear in our hearts. It was a sure sign that one of our beloved hometown boys had been killed, and everyone mourned, because everyone was family.

Those were hard times. People picked up coal by the railroad track to keep heat going in their wood-burning stoves in the wintertime. Everyone had a cow and a victory garden. The cow's fresh milk and Granny's black-eyed peas tasted pretty good to me. Granddaddy came in to the same supper every night. He crumbled his cornbread from lunch into a big round glass and filled it with Bossie's fresh milk, strained by one of Granny's clean cup towels.

The thrill of my life was when we sat on the porch in the cool of the evening and listened to Granddaddy's stories. His favorite story was told again and again.

"There was this preacher holding a revival under a brush arbor," Granddaddy said, with a twinkle in his eye. "He was really getting after it and suddenly prayed, 'Oh Lord, send the fire just now.' Some mean boys were behind the arbor and set the brush on fire. The preacher happened to look back and shouted, 'O God, I didn't mean it!'"

At the story's conclusion, Granddaddy laughed and laughed.

I also loved going to church. Granny took a quilt to make a pallet under the summer revival tent. Going to sleep smelling the rich brown earth while singing hymns of praise was the last thing I remembered before awakening the next morning cuddled up on Granny's goose featherbed.

A dry-goods store, a grocery store, the post office, and the local movie theater, The Rialto, were located on Main Street. One day, Granddaddy bought what he called a "parasol" for me at the dry-goods store, where the ladies bought chickenfeed in pretty flour sacks, which would be used as material for dresses. I paraded up and down Main Street twirling my new parasol, feeling as important as Eleanor Roosevelt.

Everyone in my eighth-grade class brought lunch in a syrup bucket. Most of them contained biscuits with leftover bacon or gravy from breakfast. It was hard not to choke sometimes, especially if you had fried potatoes between the biscuits, and there was always a long line waiting for a drink.

But though they were tough, the years passed quickly. I had my eyes set on a tall, lanky, handsome boy, and started meeting him at the town's little movie house. Any movie with Hop-Along Cassidy or Tex Ritter in it was a must-see movie. One time, Emmitt put his arm around the back of my seat and a smart-aleck kid went home and told his mother, who made a big stink about it. I didn't get to go to the movies for a long time.

Emmitt gave me a little heart locket the year we graduated, one day before he had to go to the army. I watched until the big Greyhound bus had carried him so far away I could no longer see it, and then I cried and cried.

When he came home on furlough, he brought me a ring with a tiny little diamond in it. He said it was the best the army PX had, and when he gave it to me, we talked of getting married someday soon. It was so hard to tell him goodbye. That was 1946. The years have passed quickly. Fifty-six years of married life later, I hold that little heart locket in my hand. Our grandchildren *ooh* and *ahh* over it. My teenage granddaughters see a packet of faded letters tied together with a ribbon in my old trunk and Traci picks one up.

"They're love letters from Granddad when he was in the army!" she exclaims. "Can we read them Mawmaw? Can we read them, please?"

"Of course," I say. I want them to know what a real man's love is like.

They have tears. Then they hear my grandmother's mantel clock chime and I tell them about how I found the clock while going through Granny's things. I show them Granddaddy's torn and tattered Bible. I can still see it on my granddaddy's knees, and I can still hear him pray his heart out to God in that little country church.

Memories still linger in the garden of my heart . . . precious memories from a slice of Americana that will never be again. Life in that era was a blessing for a lifetime to me, and I wouldn't have missed it for the world.

Melrose, New Mexico

Population: 736

Origins of the Town's Name

*A*ccording to some Melrose residents, the village of Melrose was originally called "Fiddler's Draw." Further investigation proves the name was later changed to "Brownhorn." This information is based on the story of two ranchers: Lonnie Horn and "Wildhorse" Brown. As the story goes, the two ranches were adjacent to one another and shared one mailbox. The mailbox was placed at the railroad crossing, which later became known as Brown-Horn. In 1905, the Santa Fe Railroad requested the village name be changed to Melrose. By 1906, the railroad had built its line through town, begun construction on a roundhouse, and had the name Melrose approved for the post office.

Though homesteaders began trickling into the area as early as 1900, the majority of Melrose's residents arrived in 1906 and 1907. At that time, homesteaders were allowed only 160 acres, but in 1912, the Homestead Act was changed so that dry-land ranches could have as much as 320 acres. In order to "prove up" on their claim, for a period of five years, homesteaders had to live at least six months of the year on their claim. Filing fees were $16.

In the early 1900s, farmers new to the area were diligent workers, but the land was unforgiving and many were not very successful in their endeavors. Noting the problem, the government sent out instruction bulletins that explained requirements for farming arid lands. In no time, broomcorn became a profitable crop, and at one time, Melrose was known as one of the broomcorn capitals of the world. In 1957, former president Dwight Eisenhower visited Curry County to assess the damage a drought had brought to the region. ॐ

Town Facts

First incorporated • Melrose was incorporated in 1916.

Transportation • In the beginning, residents got around by means of horse and wagon. Today, automobiles and pickup trucks are the chief mode of transportation.

Industry • In the early days, farming and ranching kept the town prosperous. Farming remains the mainstay, though the recent drought has caused many residents to relocate.

Location • Melrose village is located in Curry County, in eastern New Mexico, on U.S. Highway 84, about thirty-five miles west of the Texas line.

Places of note • Just a few miles from Melrose, in the small town of Clovis, is a "practice" bombing range used by the Cannon Air Force Base.

A large, popular fruit stand, located on the highway that leads to Melrose, attracts many tourists with a variety of produce.

Famous faces • William Denby Hanna, a renowned animator and producer, was born in Melrose on July 14, 1910. Hanna was the animator behind classic cartoons such as Yogi Bear, The Flintstones, and Scooby-Doo. Together with Joseph Barbera, Hanna was the dominant force in American cartooning for more than half a century, including the creation of Tom and Jerry, which won a record seven Academy Awards.

Local attractions • Old Timer's Day, a well-attended annual event, is held in the city park every August. Anyone who ever lived in Melrose is invited to come on down and chat about the "good ol' days." A parade and lots of food add to the incentive, and many former Melrose residents return. Melrose also sponsors an annual summer rodeo.

My Mother's Mirror

by Gin Rowledge | *North Stamford, Connecticut*

I AM THREE. Mom takes me into her bedroom with the crisp white curtains and chenille bedspread. She picks up the ivory hand mirror from atop the shiny mahogany dresser and holds it in front of my face.

"Sister, see how beautiful your new haircut is!"

I look into the round beveled mirror expecting a miracle. I look like the boy on the Buster Brown shoebox. I stare at my blue eyes and straight blond hair. I had thought the cut would give me dark curls like my brother's.

At five, I start first grade with blue ribbons tied to hanks of hair on top of my head. Mother again takes down the ivory mirror. We gaze together into the silver circle. She caresses the freckles on my nose. I stroke her brown hair and marvel at how she holds her bun against her neck with the wire pins.

I am eight, starting the first day of fourth grade in a red plaid dress, which Mother sewed while the family slept. I use the mirror to check the length of my braids. They are tightly held at the ends with tan rubber bands to keep them neat for the school day.

At eleven, my hair is pulled back and hangs to my shoulders. For the first day of seventh grade, Mother has made a brown-and-turquoise dress with a ruffled white eyelet yoke. I like my hair and the way the yoke makes my budding breasts look. The mirror is friendlier this time.

I am twelve when my favorite cousin gives me a Toni home perm. Shocked by the curly top and afraid of Father's reaction, I lash out at my cousin for ruining my hair. I don't realize that a bad hairdo grows out in just two weeks.

I am thirteen, going on a movie date with my best friend, Bob. We will meet on the bus and each pay our own way. I use Mom's "Betsy Ross" treadle machine to make myself a gray cotton skirt with a ruffle on the bottom. I check my hair with the mirror. I hope he notices how my clean hair shines in the sun.

When I am fifteen, my cousin forgives my meanness and gives me a "body wave." I wash and set it every night with bobby pins. I must be ready for the ride to high school in my brother's blue Model-A truck at 7:30 each morning. We pick up our best friends for the seven-mile ride and all pile into the narrow seat.

I work at a ladies' clothing shop nights and Saturdays when I am sixteen. My mother no longer sews for me. I am happy that she has made a navy-blue silk dress with pink roses for herself. I see how pretty she looks as she combs her long salt-and-pepper hair. She checks her bun for stray wisps with the mirror and I notice how yellowed the ivory mirror is becoming.

I am seventeen and in love. I worry because Mom seems tired. With her help, I remake my junior prom dress from an off-the-shoulder style to a halter top for the senior prom. The dress cost twenty-five dollars last year and I cannot buy a new one. I pin, curl, spray, and pray. With the mirror, I check the back of my head and note my daring bare back.

I graduate on a warm June evening. Childhood is over. My mom has terminal breast cancer. I tenderly brush her hair and bring her the mirror. Side by side, we look into the clear glass. Her wrinkled yellow pallor and graying hair contrast with my smooth tanned skin and sun-streaked blond hair. We both have blue eyes. Hers look to the past and mine to the future.

I am eighteen and all grown up, I think. I elope with my high school sweetheart in my bargain-sale six-dollar gray suit, sheer nylon blouse, white velvet hat, and high heels. I pack while Dad is at work. My heart is heavy as I include the mirror.

Today, I am a widow. The mirror reveals fine lines, wrinkles, and an old lady's neck. I think it is, perhaps, time to pass the mirror on to my daughter. I want her to see her own smooth, radiant face reflected in my mother's mirror on her wedding day. ૮ঙ

Pelican Summer

by Melinda Fausey | *Merritt Island, Florida*

"Mom, you can't sell this!" The carved wooden pelican sat in the middle of the yard, towering over the other knickknacks my parents were selling in their garage sale. The huge five-bedroom house was too big for them now that their three children had grown up and moved away, and much to my dismay, a sizable chunk of my childhood was now strewn across the lawn.

"You can have it," my mother replied with a sweet smile. She obviously remembered the story behind the pelican, and why I was so fond of the cracked and peeling wooden statue she had purchased so long ago both as a decoration and as a memento of the best summer of my childhood. I picked up the pelican, and bright white flecks of paint drifted to the ground. Looking into its clear yellow-beaded eyes, memories came rushing back to me, reminding me of a less complicated time ...

❧

Civilization ended at the end of our street. One well-worn dirt trail wove into the thick Florida swampland, warning adults of possible threats and danger, but beckoning us kids to a potential playground of adventure.

We all gathered at the head of the trail, ready to again explore the internal heart of the swamp, hoping to spy a panther. We'd seen our share of reclusive alligators, and rattlesnakes and cottonmouths were almost a daily sight, but we'd never had the privilege of seeing a panther.

Our plan was to climb the giant Australian pines and wait for the mysterious cat to walk beneath us. We'd seen her paw prints in the mud after a rain shower. We knew she was there. And we were desperate to catch a glimpse.

"Okay, are we all here?" Peter, at thirteen, was the oldest of our little group of friends. He pointed his finger at each one of us, silently counting Robin, Kippy—Peter's little sister—Chris, and Patrick, my younger brother. And me, of course.

"Let's go," I said, anxious to see the elusive big cat.

With a solemn nod, Peter turned and disappeared into the thick brush. We followed single file, swatting at mosquitoes and pushing aside low-hanging branches from the scrub palms edging the path. I found a long, sturdy stick and used it to beat the bushes and to occasionally poke my brother when I thought he moved too slowly.

By the time we reached the towering strand of Australian pines, it was hot. My long hair hung in wet strands down my back, and had I not been such a tomboy, I would've put it up into a ponytail. My brother followed Peter's lead and took off his shirt, draping it over his shoulder.

"I don't think I can climb this tree," Kippy said, squinting toward the tops of the pines. At nine years of age, Kippy was the youngest, and we had been afraid she might do something like this.

Peter sighed for all of us. "I'll give you a push," he said.

After a while, we were all up in three different trees. I climbed up one a little away from the others, wanting to be as far away from my pesky brother as possible.

Below us was a wide area of the trail leading to the edge of the water. Tall brown cattails stood as sentinels around the opening to the algae-coated water. This is where we'd seen the cat's tracks.

I was beginning to lose interest in the whole ordeal when something in the water caught my eye. A pelican, white as an otherworldly specter, glided across the deceptively calm water. I shifted to get a better view, ignoring the hard knots that jammed into my bottom.

I was as mesmerized as if it had truly been a ghost. Pelicans typically like to fly over the nearby Atlantic Ocean. We'd never seen one in the swamp before.

As it swam toward shore, everything grew eerily quiet. Even the breeze whispering through the towering pines hushed, as if watching this out-of-place newcomer with heightened expectation.

The pelican blinked, and even from my perch high in the trees, I can remember how it flicked its eyes open and shut, and tilted its long beak just a little to one side.

Suddenly, a violent thrashing disrupted the water, and the pelican beat its wings frantically as an alligator snapped its powerful jaws in the air. The pelican shot across the surface of the water, and the alligator again lunged and missed.

In the trees, we were silent, holding our breath.

The pelican, against all odds, made it to shore, and as one, the six of us exhaled.

Kippy began to clap. "Yay, pelican!"

The sound startled the alligator and it slipped underwater into the murky depths. However, the pelican tilted its head, as though listening to Kippy's exuberance. After several moments, when it still made no move, I climbed down from the tree and cautiously approached the huge bird.

"It's okay, I won't hurt you," I crooned as I drew near. Again, it cocked its head, listening to my voice. I reached out and touched its pale orange beak. It didn't flinch, didn't jerk away. I stroked its neck with my fingertips, wondering at the softness of its bright white feathers. It was then that I realized the pelican was blind. Cataracts clouded its eyes with a hazy fog.

"He's blind," I called back to the others, who scrambled quickly down from the trees.

"How do you know?" my brother asked.

"He's got the same thing Grandpa had. I think he needs an operation." I thought a minute, then made up my mind. "I'm bringing him home."

Patrick snorted. "How do you think you're going to get that thing all the way home?"

I picked the pelican up. He was heavy. I struggled to carry him a few feet, then set him down.

"Maybe mom will come and look at him," I said and started down the path, intent on somehow finding help for this poor creature. Surely, he couldn't survive long without his sight. And I wasn't going to let him die after he'd miraculously survived the alligator attack. "I'll be right back. Stay with him."

Instead of staying put, the pelican begin to follow me. In fact, he followed me the whole way home, responding to my voice with tentative, slapping steps.

My mother was in the front yard, pulling weeds from the flower-bed when we stepped from the path. She stood up as she saw me walk slowly across the yard, the pelican at my heels.

"Mindy, what on earth is that?"

She knew what it was. It was obviously a pelican.

I ignored her question. "It's blind, Mom, look at his eyes."

My mother bent down and peered closely at the bird. She sighed, then scratched her head.

"Let me make some phone calls." She stood up and stared at the pelican, raking her hands through her long, wavy hair. Then she smiled at me. My mother was beautiful. "You and your animals," she said, ruffling my hair.

An hour later, a white van pulled into our driveway. A woman from an animal rescue organization stepped out and took my pelican in her arms.

"Will you make him better?" I asked, trying not to cry.

The lady smiled at me. "I sure will. He'll get the treatment he needs and we'll take him back to the ocean where he belongs."

The pelican blinked. It seemed as if he were winking at me, letting me know that he would be okay, that he had, after all, survived a brush with an alligator. Convinced he would be fine and that he was in good hands, I swallowed my tears. With all the courage I could muster, I winked back.

Saving It for Good

by Karen Commings | *Penbrook, Pennsylvania*

READY TO WASH MY FACE, I look in the mirror above the bathroom sink. My eyes are tired. The lines around them, and the pouches of skin that hang like discarded purses from the corners of my mouth, look just like my grandmother's. I am two years older than she is in the last photo I took of her with my Brownie box-camera in 1958, when I was twelve years old. In the picture, she is sitting on a chair at her chrome and Formica kitchen table opening a Christmas present. Several Santa and Mrs. Claus salt and pepper shakers populate the table behind her.

My grandmother wore her dark brown, waist-length hair tied back in a bun, and short clumps of it would become free and drift into her face. Uncomfortable about being photographed, Gram had laughed and brushed back a lock of hair dangling over her forehead as I snapped the picture. Knee-high nylons were still on the invention horizon, so Gram wore her regular nylons rolled down over an elastic garter to a point just below her knees where her calves functioned like hosiery guardrails to prevent them from continuing the trip down her legs. Gram's rolled-down hose were noticeable only

◄○►

when she sat down and her dress rode up to reveal them. I immortalized them on film.

Buying gifts for Gram was a challenge. If we spent money on something out-of-the-ordinary, she put it away, never wore it until some special occasion warranted it. None of the occasions ever did, until Gram's oldest daughter, my mother, died at the age of fifty-two.

"I'll save this for good," Gram always said as she opened colorfully wrapped packages containing items of clothing we had hand selected. When the crumpled paper and empty boxes filled the trash, my grandmother refolded the garments and placed them in a dresser drawer where they stayed for years, sometimes decades.

On the morning of my mother's funeral, she took out a slip we had bought her at some point in the ancient past.

"I was saving this for good," she said, trying to shake loose the creases, embossed into the slip's silky fabric from eons of being folded. Her oldest daughter had died, and this was the occasion to which she would wear the "good" slip, under a dress that she had also "saved for good."

My grandmother never went anywhere special. She never traveled, never went to parties or other social gatherings, except the occasional holiday meal at our house. Her days were occupied with earning a meager living by cleaning government offices. Her evenings were spent caring for the myriad birds she kept in her second-floor apartment. My mother's funeral was about as "good" as it got.

Within days after my mother's death, my grandmother's three surviving children, who converged on Pennsylvania for the first time in more than a decade, decided to send her and her pet birds via airplane to California with my uncle. I saw Gram only once in California. Her cotton housedresses had been exchanged for knit pants and polyester blouses. Short, gray, permed hair replaced her thick, long black locks. I don't know if she ever wore the "good" slip or dress again. My uncle sent her to my aunt in Alaska shortly thereafter, where she died peacefully in her sleep nine years after my mother died.

Growing up, I swore I'd never be like my parents. It never occurred to me that I might become my grandmother. I look in the mirror again and see more than the lines on her face. So, I slide into a pair of pants instead of my ratty, but comfortable, blue jeans. I replace the sweatshirt I'm wearing with a color-coordinated turtleneck and sweater. I spritz on some perfume, a light scent that won't elicit dirty looks or nasty comments from those who might be allergic. I put on enough mascara to keep me from looking like a lashless lizard, and pick out some lipstick from the dozen or so containers collecting dust in a pottery bowl next to the sink. I go for a two-stage application, which should outlast the first doughnut and cup of coffee, maybe the second.

I've had enough cups of coffee already to bolster the gross national product of Columbia, so, what am I saving it for? I spread a light coating of lipstick onto my lips, and am suddenly grateful that I'm going grocery shopping and not attending a funeral. ꙮ

A Precious Rose

by Gayle Sorensen Stringer | *Tyler, Minnesota*

MUCH LIKE LAURA INGALLS WILDER, I grew up on the undulating prairies of southwestern Minnesota. Our dairy farm rested just seven miles north of Tyler—population 1,069. I was schooled, churched, and indelibly influenced by the folks of my hometown community.

My grandmother still lives there. Long widowed, she now resides in a retirement village. She and my grandfather spent their prime north of town, farming and raising four children. Although much of my family has dispersed from the area due to economic strains, it is good to know she is still holding down the fort and guarding our place in the town's history. I like to visit her when I can, although 1,000 miles and my own family and responsibilities provide plenty of obstacles to nostalgic travel. Still, luck is mine from time to time, and I find myself swaddled in my grandmother's familiar ambience and gorging greedily on memories produced from stacks of old photo albums and scrapbooks.

During one such episode, I happened upon a carefully preserved rose in a certain scrapbook. Beneath the withered blossom, my grandmother's meticulously penned caption read, *"A PRECIOUS ROSE.*

Little Gayle walked all the way down here on a hot August day carrying this rose in her hand to give to me. She was only five years old. 1966."

I smiled as my mind drifted back.

❧

I sat looking at the vase of homegrown roses on the kitchen table. They represented many hues, but my favorites were the apricots.

"Orangey-pink and so sweet," I murmured.

"What did you say, honey?" my mother asked from her place at the sink.

"I said I like these the best," I said, pointing to the apricot blossoms.

"Pick out your favorite and give it to your grandma when you go to play with Lisa today," Mom suggested. "Aunt Janet will be here soon to get you. I have a few chores to do in the barn, so wait here until she comes."

The screen door slammed shut behind Mom, and I busied myself with my selection. I settled on one of the apricots and waited for my aunt's arrival.

"I hope Lisa doesn't ask me that same old question, again," I said out loud. Lisa was my cousin from Des Moines, Iowa. She and her family were here for a visit and staying at my grandparents' farm. I enjoyed all the things my cousin and I did together, like climbing trees and searching for newborn kittens and collecting pretty stones, I just didn't like her initial question. Every day, when I arrived to play, Lisa asked, "Did you walk here?"

I felt like a baby when I had to answer, "No."

Suddenly, I had an idea. I plucked Grandma's rose from the vase and banged through the screen door. I skipped down the winding driveway of my family's farm, carefully clutching the flower.

When I reached the end of the driveway, I stopped and peered up the country road in the direction of Grandma's farm. Lying three miles north and west, I couldn't see it, but I was sure I knew the way. Cautiously, I stepped onto the pavement. My parents' warnings about walking along the road echoed in my mind, but the thorns sticking my thumb seemed to urge me on. The tar felt firm and smelled hot. Butterflies fluttered overhead, and flies buzzed past my ears.

"Maybe I should walk in the ditch," I thought out loud. I picked my way down the steep decline and began swooshing through the tall grass. The sun warmed my head and arms, the wind puffed, and the fragrances of rich farmland and cut hay filled my nostrils. Wild flowers winked in the grass and birds chuckled. Occasionally, a car whizzed by on the road above, but no one noticed the five-year-old girl in the bottom of the ditch. I felt like I was on a grand adventure. I felt very grown-up.

But after a while, wading through the rough grasses made my skin itch. Strands of blond hair pulled loose from my ponytail and blew in a bothersome way around my face. My forehead and cheeks felt moist, and my mouth, dry. An irritating stone found its way into my shoe. I sat down to dump the stone from my sneaker and dreamed of cold lemonade and homemade cookies as I watched the industry of an ant mound.

"Ants are so busy," I sighed and almost burst into tears. But then my gaze caught one particular ant hefting a load twice its size up toward the ant mound. It seemed an impossible task for such a small creature, but *it never gave up.*

I pulled on my shoe and struggled to my feet. Shielding my eyes with my hand, I looked down the empty stretch of highway. Then, I trudged on. At last, I reached the intersection, and from there I could see the barns and silos of my grandparents' farm. Popping out of the ditch like a gopher, I dashed across the road and ran the rest of the distance. Proudly, I skipped down my grandparents' driveway.

"There she is!" Lisa shouted as she ran toward me.

"I've been looking high and low for you," Aunt Janet said as she leaned in relief against her car door.

"I just wanted to make sure I brought you the right flower," I said, presenting my grandma with the bedraggled rose.

"It's beautiful," Grandma said, "but don't ever do anything like this again!"

She called my mom to report my safety and then served the longed-for lemonade and cookies.

"Did you walk here?" Lisa asked.

"Yep," I grinned.

Grandma glanced at the sad-looking rose adorning her favorite vase and smiled. "Well, I guess all's well that ends well."

Today, Grandma snapped the rings of the scrapbook open and handed the page to me. "You should have this," she said. "Keep it to remember your inner strength and the wonderful times we have shared."

And I do. ∽

The Trunk in the Attic

by John R. Gugel | *Muskego, Wisconsin*

IN THE WEEKS following our father's death, my brother searched the attic of our parents' home. He was not looking for anything in particular but was just making an informal inventory of its contents.

On one of his ventures into the attic, in a far corner, stuck in a dormer and wedged between the ceiling joist and the floor, Mike found an old locked trunk. He didn't think much about it at the time, but since his daughter and son-in-law collect old trunks, he made a mental note to check it out later.

Several weeks later, he made another trip into the attic. This time he tried to move the trunk. It proved to be heavier than he had imagined, giving every indication of being quite full. Curious, he pried the lock to investigate. Inside, he found one of the most wonderful treasures a person could hope to discover—our legacy.

Our birth mother had died of a stroke in the days following my birth, in 1946. My father, distraught over her death, suddenly found himself a young widower with three boys to raise on his own.

A year later, at a church convention in Chicago, he ran into a woman he had known several years before. She worked at Valparaiso

University and invited him to a Crusaders football game that fall. They corresponded, and four months later were married in her hometown of Mattoon, Illinois.

Our new mother was wonderful. She stepped right in and took on the job of raising us as her own. (We, of course, were perfect angels.) She often told the story of how she got married one day, rode the train home the next, and on the third day was hauling laundry downstairs to the basement while Dad went back to work. There was no time for a honeymoon.

I never could understand why fairy tales often told about "wicked" stepmothers. That was just not part of our "step" experience. Yet, as much as I loved my new mom, I felt something was missing from my life. I grew up a bit jealous of other children who had their mom for their whole life.

When my brother pried open the trunk, he was not prepared for what he discovered. It was filled with my birth mother's belongings. Apparently, Dad put them all away in the trunk when he remarried. He saved them out of love and respect for the wife he lost, and hid them away out of love and respect for the wife he gained.

Inside were clothes, scrapbooks, photo albums, and various odds and ends, items accumulated over a life cut short.

The photographs, the oldest dating to 1926, were in mint condition, not having seen the light of day for more than fifty years. They revealed a beautiful young woman who was often at the center of her circle of friends, vivacious, fun-loving, high-spirited. There were pictures with her friends from summers spent at Camp Cleghorn in northern Wisconsin, and numerous family snapshots. One album documented her bicycle trip through England with her sister, my Aunt Edna, in the summer of 1936. Imagine, in those days, two young women traveling on their own like that!

She devoted one scrapbook to her wedding—every card and gift label found its way into her scrapbook, which served as a chronicle for her various bridal showers and the wedding itself. In addition, the trunk held the patterns and swatches of cloth for the bridesmaids' dresses and her wedding gown—all of which she sewed herself.

But the biggest surprise—one that brought tears to my eyes—was the most precious fifty feet of 8mm film on this planet. The color film had been shot on the day of my parents' wedding, as they were getting ready to leave Grandma's house for the church. And, when we found an ancient projector to play it on, there she was on the screen. Imagine the thrill I felt when, at age fifty-two, I saw my mother for the first time in my life. She was radiant, warm, loving, laughing, hugging—there was even a shot of her giving Dad a kiss.

We grew up in my parents' house under the attic. My bedroom was just feet from the attic door. When my folks were gone for an evening, we kids would sneak up the stairs and play hide-and-seek with the only light coming through the dormer window.

We never knew how close we were to such a treasure. Maybe it is just as well. As we grow older, we cherish that which constitutes our legacy more than when we are children. And we will never know if Dad was going to tell us about the trunk. My guess is that he wanted to but never knew how to bring up the subject. Did he ever open the trunk? I don't know the answer to that question. I am just so grateful to my brother for snooping around in that attic. ⁀

Grandma's Boat

by Lester Tucker | *Willacoochee, Georgia*

I STARTED WRITING POETRY thirty-six years ago, in the fifth grade. A few months ago, I was going through boxes stored in my attic and found a box containing my old notebooks and journals. Reminiscing about young love and the girls who inspired a lot of my poems, I came across a poem entitled "Grandma's Boat" by A. L. Smith.

Mr. Smith was our next-door neighbor in my hometown of Willacoochee, Georgia. There was a footpath from our back door to his, carved out by six little feet from our daily visits. I remember waking up and running next door in my pajamas to eat breakfast with him and his wife, Miss Gussie, almost every day, from the time I was old enough to walk to age four. My father was pastor at the Methodist church, and though we moved every four or five years to towns across South Georgia, Mr. Smith would come stay with us for a few days, two or three times a year. After Miss Gussie died, when I was seven, he stayed for a week each visit. We considered him our adopted grandfather.

During one visit, when I was eleven years old, he helped me write a poem for a literature homework assignment. On his next visit, he gave me the poem "Grandma's Boat," and I let him read the poetry I had written. The highlight of every visit for the next nine years, before his death, would be for him to read my poetry and encourage me to continue writing.

Sitting on the floor beside this box of old notebooks, memories of him flooded my mind as I held the aged paper on which the poem was typed. "Grandma's Boat" carries me back to the time of the Civil War and the struggles of a Confederate soldier's wife raising three kids while her husband was off at war, where he was killed. She would have to cross a river in a makeshift boat to go work in a farmer's field all day, and her pay was a peck of shelled corn. Coming home one day, after a long day in the field, Grandma got to the river to find the boat had drifted to the other side. She removed her clothes and prayed that God would help her get across so she could get home to her children. Her faith was as strong as her will and she made it across. Mr. Smith ended the poem knowing one day he would see her in heaven and see Jesus standing beside Grandma's boat.

As I finished reading, I thought of my three grandsons and how the oldest at age five is already showing an interest in poetry as we make up stories and he struggles to rhyme words. I can only hope that I will be a positive influence in their lives as Mr. Smith was in mine, and one day they, too, might be going through some old boxes and find a poem I gave to them, and enjoy the memories of time spent with me.

I don't believe there is any treasure worth as much as the memories we make spending time with those we love. I thank God for allowing Mr. Smith to have been part of my life and look forward to one day taking a ride with him in Grandma's boat. ♋

Willacoochee, Georgia

Population: 1,434

Places of Note

*W*illacoochee's "No Name Bar" was mentioned in columns written by the late journalist Lewis Grizzard. In the early 1960s, the leading industry in Atkinson County was McCranie Brothers Wood Preserving. This company can be found along Highway 82, on Willacoochee's east side. These days, McCranie Turpentine is a prominent local historical site. Old Fashion Day, held the first Saturday in July, has plenty of attraction for locals and visitors alike, including a Friday evening dance and vendors' booths.

How the Town Was Named

*T*he town was originally known as Danialsville, after a family who lived in the area, but the name was eventually changed to Willacoochee, after a nearby river with the same name. There is some discrepancy about what the word Willacoochee means. While all Willacoochee residents note the word Willacoochee is derived from a Native American term, some claim the word means "little river" and others believe it means "home of the wildcat."

Town Facts

First incorporated • Willacoochee was incorporated on November 12, 1889

Location • Willacoochee is located in south-central Georgia, along Highway 82—twenty-eight miles east of Tifton, seventeen miles southwest of Douglas, forty-seven miles northeast of Valdosta, and forty-two miles west of Waycross. Bordered by the Alapaha River on the south side and the Willacoochee River on the west, Willacoochee residents take advantage of the area's prime hunting and fishing land.

Transportation • Willacoochee, the first town chartered in Atkinson County, was also the first town in Georgia to own a railroad. Following an Act of Legislature, in 1889, the city was set at "one-half mile each way from the Brunswick and Western Railroad Depot in said town." Additionally, when townsfolk learned that the Georgia and Florida Railroad that runs north and south through Willacoochee would be abandoned, city leaders moved to purchase eighteen miles of track and right-of-way from Willacoochee to Nashville to preserve the success of two industries: Langboard Inc. and Pasta America.

Industry • From its inception, agriculture has been important in Willacoochee. In fact, agriculture and agribusiness were the dominant area industries until well into the 1990s. When U.S. Highway 82 was revamped into a four-lane freeway, the little town of Willacoochee instantly became a passageway between nearby Interstates 75 and 95. Seemingly overnight, industry boomed and has continued in that vein. Additionally, private industry has invested more than $110 million and has provided jobs for nearly 1,000 employees, which have been a vital part in boosting economic growth.

The Coin

by Al Serradell | *Rush Springs, Oklahoma*

I was helping Mom pack for her umpteenth hospital stay when she pressed the coin into the palm of my right hand. It was a silver dollar, minted in 1885. She said her father had given it to her about fifty years ago, after the family moved to California from Oklahoma in the early 1940s. Handing down the coin was a tradition by then. My grandfather, she explained, had received the dollar as a gift from his parents.

And now it had been passed on to me. I accepted my legacy with a bittersweet mixture of pride and dread. No doubt Mom's real motivation behind the gesture had more to do with time. And inevitability. She knew she wasn't going to beat the cancer. It was no longer a matter of her not responding well to treatment. At this point, the doctors were merely chasing the disease, attacking each isolated mass before it could spring up somewhere else.

That night, I put the coin away. I couldn't bear to look at it then, so I slipped it into my strongbox with all of my other important papers and belongings. I figured I'd examine the treasure in time, after the grieving process was over and life resumed with a new, happier pattern.

One night, about a week later, I returned home exhausted. It had been a long, sad day, beginning with a hectic eight-hour stretch at the university's public relations office where I worked. I spent the last few hours of my day at the hospital, visiting Mom.

As usual, I stayed with her until the evening's medication had been administered and she drifted off to sleep. Only then did I feel confident that she would be okay for one more night.

I was more annoyed than surprised that evening to find my apartment door unlocked. No doubt I had forgotten the morning ritual in my mad rush to get to work. With a laugh, I thought of all the things that had slipped my mind recently, everything from setting the alarm clock to turning off the stove after cooking dinner.

"You're becoming dangerous, Al," I scolded as I entered my apartment. My facetious attitude morphed into disbelief the moment I stepped across the threshold and saw my now bare desk. My keyboard and monitor were missing. Looking around, I noticed my TV and stereo system were also missing; speakers, too. I swallowed a lungful of rage: I'd been robbed.

My feet dragging, I moved into the bedroom and saw further evidence of the robbery. My closet door lay open, suitcases and clothes pulled down from the top shelf. Every drawer had been ransacked, the contents emptied onto the hardwood floor.

Then I saw the strongbox in the middle of the bed. . . . With sinking dread, I remembered the coin my mother had given me just last week. The horrible probability that it also had been stolen pushed away all other thoughts. My heart wedged inside my throat, I rushed to the metal box and searched frantically for the leather pouch that housed the precious gift. It was gone. I felt like screaming. This wasn't fair! As if the family hadn't had enough to deal with, now this.

My already fuzzy mind must've gotten the best of me, because I don't remember contacting the police or waiting while they dusted my apartment for fingerprints. I wasn't even aware of time passing.

Later, as I walked the police to the door, I seemed to snap out of my fugue, though my thoughts still focused on the missing coin.

Before they left, one of the officers shook my hand and tried to lighten the situation by remarking, "At least the thief or thieves left you some change on your kitchen table."

The importance of his words didn't register until later, after I'd showered and got ready for bed. *Change?* I turned back the comforter. *On the kitchen table?* Could it be . . . ? Then, like a light clicking on inside my brain, it all came back to me. I'd taken the coin out that morning while speaking to my brother on the phone. I'd told him about the gift but couldn't remember the year of the minting.

Now totally awake, I hurried to the kitchen, to the scene of "the crime." Sure enough, there, in the middle of the table, surrounded by stacks of "dummy" brochures I'd been preparing for work, I spotted the coin resting on its leather pouch. Dropping into a chair, I breathed deeply as a great sadness and fear that I had lost a family heirloom left my body. I don't know how long I sat there, but it was long enough to utter a genuine prayer of thanks.

Despite the robbery, I felt lucky. None of the stolen items really mattered. They were just things—electronic equipment, easily replaced.

An old coin might not seem like much of a legacy to some people. Not like the title to an estate or a collection of priceless gems. But to me, that silver dollar represented a gift beyond monetary value. It connected me to my past, to a long line of ancestors—proud survivors.

More important, I'd become part of a history that would continue long after I was gone, a gift for whole new generations to come. ∽

Grandma's House

by Connie Koopman Pettersen | *Madison, South Dakota*

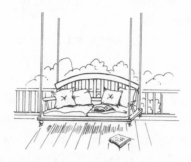

I KNOW IT'S FINALLY SPRING when I see the spotted brownish-gray mourning doves returning to my yard. Their low, mournful cooing not only signals the end of winter, but also takes me back on a nostalgic journey to the 1950s and visits to my grandma's house on the southeast edge of Madison, South Dakota.

Grandma, Anna Koopman, a widowed daughter of German immigrants, lived on a graveled street, in a white cottage canopied by giant elms. Neighbors were nearby, yet it was as close to a farm as you could get and still remain within the city limits.

I was used to the city noises in St. Paul, Minnesota—fire engines blaring, streetcars clicking across cobbled streets, and the shrilling of factory whistles. A small, quiet town was a novelty.

At Grandma's, I'd awake to the gentle cooing of mourning doves outside her upstairs spare-room window. I loved those country-sounding doves. Combined with the sweet fragrance of spring lilacs wafting through the open window, these sounds and aromas were imprinted on my senses as part of rural Madison and visits with Grandma.

I remember lying in bed upstairs, listening to the town wake up—a persistent dog yipping, the soft rumbling of a distant train and lonesome drone of its faraway whistle, roosters crowing from the neighbor's chicken coop, and the comforting *tick-tick-tick*ing of the bedside Big Ben alarm clock.

The sound of a rattling stove lid from downstairs indicated Grandma was up. Water would slosh in the pail from the kitchen pump and I'd picture her filling her enormous tin teakettle to heat for washing up or doing dishes in the white metal basin.

"Breakfast's ready," she'd yell, and I'd come down to a bowl of hot oatmeal with cream and brown sugar, or a slab of bacon with fried eggs, toast, and jam. In my mind's eye, Grandma still stands by her black-and-gray woodstove holding a wooden spoon in hand. Her blue eyes twinkle behind gold wire-rimmed glasses as she greets me, "Good morning! Wipe the Sandman from your eyes—the day won't wait for sleepyheads!"

Her waist-length gray hair was worn braided and twisted into a bun. A full calico apron covered her faded housedress, one of two Grandma Anna owned—a black one with red roses and a navy blue with white polka dots. I remember the warm, safe feeling of her lap, my head against her ample bosom, the starch of her white lace collar scratching my cheek.

Sometimes Grandma would settle with me in a creaking wooden rocker. She'd hum and sing her favorite hymns, "Rock of Ages" or "Amazing Grace," and tell of our heavenly home and God's love for me. Sometimes she'd read Bible stories about David and Goliath or Noah's Ark. At Grandma's knee I felt the Lord's presence, for Grandma knew how to talk to God.

Grandma's kitchen was the center of activity. Meals were served on an oak table with legs carved like animal paws and covered with a floral patterned oilcloth. On special occasions Grandma used hand-crocheted tablecloths. Her white metal cabinet held yellow and pink etched Davy Crockett juice glasses and chipped, mismatched china covered with fascinating little spider-web veins. My favorite white china teacup had a painted pink rose on it. Occasionally, I'd be allowed to sip warm milk laced with a little tea from that special cup.

I remember fingerlike ridges on her Depression glass sugar bowl, and pewter salt and pepper shakers. Grandma's wide silver-plated flatware tasted like metal but didn't discourage me from enjoying chicken soup and yellow dumplings, homemade sauerkraut with pork ribs, or chicken with sage dressing baked in her enormous black speckled roasting pan.

Grandma's "window bread" was sliced homemade bread, amply buttered and carved with squares before being covered with strawberry jam. Her gold ceramic cookie jar held oatmeal-raisin cookies or soft molasses gingers that melted in my mouth.

Ground-level flowerboxes, outside the kitchen, contained tulips, daylilies, and ant-covered peony bushes. No matter how hard I shook those pink and white peonies outside, we still found ants once the bouquet was put on the table inside.

Adjacent to the kitchen was Grandma's bedroom. It smelled like the sachets in her bureau. Puffy feather pillows and hand-stitched crazy quilts made from castoff clothing dressed her brass bed. Her round-topped square trunk held quilts, embroidered pillowcases, and crocheted doilies that smelled like mothballs. Atop her bedside table was the ever-present green jar of Mentholatum. The scents of flowers and medicine combined to make Grandma's peculiar fragrance one of distinction. She insisted it cleared her sinuses.

Alas, Grandma's house had electricity but no bathroom or running water. A major drawback was the walk to the outside privy through Grandma's bedroom lean-to. The backyard path led to a weathered two-holer, adjacent to the beautiful pink and scarlet hollyhocks that waved gently in the wind. I sacrificed privacy for a slightly open door and a view of Grandma's gardens to distract from the pungent odor.

Thankfully, those days are gone. However, even with the modern time-saving conveniences, time itself remains the commodity I have the least of in today's fast-paced world.

I can still glean moments of peaceful, soul-renewing quiet time while sipping tea from Grandma's rose-painted teacup and listening to the world wake up. This particular morning, as I talk to God, two pairs of spotted mourning doves land in my yard. I watch them cautiously search for sunflower seeds under my deck feeder and hear them cooing.

I listen. I remember. And I'm content.

Gettin' from Here to There

by Barbara Wild | *Frisco, Texas*

I REMEMBER HOW Mama hated that old car. Every time she climbed out of it, she swore she'd drive it off a cliff next time. Daddy admitted it had a couple of peculiarities, which always drove Mama into a tizzy.

"Peculiarities!" she snorted. "Running over my own bumper while driving down Main Street in plain sight of the whole town is not a peculiarity! It's embarrassing! And I suppose you think I enjoy driving all the way through town and around again so I can park in front of Curtsinger's Drug coming from the right because that . . ." She stuttered here. Mama was a proper lady, and she couldn't bring herself to say the words that accurately described what she wanted to say. ". . . that *car* won't turn to the left!"

Daddy didn't help Mama's mood by saying she should just be glad she was "gettin' from here to there," but he always said it anyway, with a sly wink at me.

He bought the 1931 Model-A for $125. It was meant to fill in until he could afford a pickup, and "fill in" stretched to quite some time. That was common in 1949 Frisco, Texas, population 700.

Necessity was served before luxury, and transportation was *usually* a tractor or a pickup. No good for plowing a cotton patch or hauling a pig to market, cars were rare. But that didn't mean folks didn't have one on their "when-that-good-crop-comes-in" wish list. It was there, right after a new tractor. A bright blue exception belonged to Miz Roach. More than eighty years old, she was deaf as a stone and practically blind. All that could be seen as she herded a '48 Buick through the streets was a pair of lace gloves with a death grip on the steering wheel and a snowy fluff of hair. There was an ongoing debate about whether she could actually see the road or just knew where she was going by virtue of muscle memory. She shouldn't have been driving anymore, but no one had the heart to make her stop. Besides, she pretty much went to the same place at the same time, and so her predictability insured public safety.

"Here comes Miz Roach, y'all," was an often-heard warning, always delivered with a grin.

That summer, a brand-new Ford sedan was raffled off. Most everybody in town choked up the dollar to buy a ticket, and then gathered around an elevated platform in the center of town for the drawing. The dark green Ford sat alongside the platform, reflecting Saturday-scrubbed faces in its shiny surface. People touched it gingerly, as if it might disappear like a soap bubble.

An official-looking gentleman looked around the crowd, pointed at me, and said, "How about you draw the ticket, young lady?"

Before I could decide if I wanted to or not, Daddy lifted me up onto the platform. I was seven that year, and knew most of the hopeful faces that smiled up at me, offering everything from ice cream to a pony if I just picked their name. As a blindfold was placed over my eyes, I wished I could get the new Ford for Mama. Then the man put my hand in a hat filled with tickets, cautioning me to pick only one. The crowd continued its good-natured bribery until I held up a ticket and the official shouted the name of the winner. It wasn't Daddy's.

A young man with slicked-down black hair hollered, hugged his equally young wife, and leaped onto the stage. He swung me in the air and gave me a quarter. I got a quarter and Mama still had to drive that old car. I felt guilty.

One Sunday, in early fall, we all got into the old car to go to church. Mama slammed the door with a look that dared anything to fall off. We didn't have a driveway, so the car sat in the yard, which was the same rich black loam as the fields. It became thick, sticky black mud with the addition of the least bit of moisture, and it was raining. Of course, the car was stuck in the stuff. Daddy got out to push, yelling at Mama to step on the gas when he shoved. Dressed in his only suit, starched white shirt, and shined shoes, he pushed and Mama gave it gas. The tires found traction somewhere, and the car took off. So did Daddy—face-first in the mud.

Mama stopped the car on the gravel road and looked back at Daddy. She was somewhere between sympathetic tears and hysterical laughter. Daddy was slinging mud from his face, getting madder by the second. Mama got herself under control, sympathy getting the upper hand, and offered to help him change clothes. He sputtered and spewed, still slinging mud, and pointed toward town. Mama said she thought Daddy wanted us to go on without him, and so we did.

Explaining why Daddy was not at church, Mama tried to be sympathetic in telling the story, but when she reached the spot in the story where Daddy pointed toward town, she started laughing, as did everybody in the congregation.

Halfway between the Affirmation of Faith and the sermon, Daddy slid quietly into the pew beside Mama. A quiet snicker fluttered around the sanctuary. Daddy grinned. He never could stay mad very long.

A few months later, the old Model-A was traded in for a pickup. Daddy got the truck at a good price because it had been a demonstrator and had a few miles on it. He also got a $100 trade-in on that old car. It made me smile when Mama and Daddy told me they stayed up all that night looking at that pickup in the moonlight.

There were many cars to follow, most much nicer than my parents had dreamed of in 1949, but none holds a special place in their memory. Mama is gone now, but the story of her and that cantankerous old Model-A is repeated time and again, and it never fails to bring smiles to now-wrinkled faces. As with all such family stories, it keeps her young in our memories and ever with us. ᖌ

Community Tub

by Betty Davis | *Clear Creek, Missouri*

ONE AFTERNOON, WHILE DRIVING through my neighborhood, a splash of bright pink and purple caught my attention and I quickly glanced into the lawn of a passing home. Immediately transfixed, I stared, misty-eyed. Not at the pink and purple petunias bobbing gaily in the late spring breeze, but rather at the galvanized tub they were planted in.

Many, many years ago, in Clear Creek, Missouri, galvanized tubs had been popular for use in bathing young children. As I thought about it, a smile crept across my face. We children were very similar to the cheerful petunias, bobbing and splashing about, at least until the year I turned eight and bath time took on an entirely different meaning.

As if time had stood still, my mind wandered back to the exact moment when the community tub became a thing of the past for me.

The day was cold—icy, snowy. Mom brought wood in for the cookstove and to get the heater in the bedroom fired up. The only time she built a fire in the bedroom heater was when she intended for us to bathe. In the beds lining the wall of the room, four little heads rolled like doubting eyes.

"Oh, no! We aren't going to take a bath are we? There's snow on the ground," I complained.

"Why should that matter? The snow won't make you clean." Mom had a matter-of-fact kind of mind.

I bolted upright in the cold air and pulled back the curtain from a nearby window. Snow was everywhere. Icicles hung like spikes from the roof and window frames. Shivering, I returned to my warm cave in the goose-feather mattress of my bed. I dreaded bathing. All those naked little bodies shoved into the same galvanized tub—at the same time—while cakes of Ivory soap floated smugly on the surface was enough to set my teeth to chattering.

Mom didn't seem to realize I no longer liked being nude in front of everyone.

Since my eighth birthday, my heart felt strange every time someone walked in on me when I was changing clothes. Though I couldn't understand it, I did not like the feeling. I was so uncomfortable, I had begun dressing under the bedcovers. Each night, I laid my gown on the bed and crawled under the blankets to dress. As I removed my clothes, each piece was laid close by so the next morning I could emerge fully dressed.

This particular Saturday, I did not get out of bed like the other children when Mom had finished pouring the water into the community tub. Without looking at me, Mom said, "Jenny, I'm glad you aren't up yet. I think your body is just getting too big to get in the tub with the other children. It's too crowded." As I said, Mom had a matter-of-fact mind.

I didn't answer, just pulled the covers over my head so I could not see the other naked bodies. After they had finished, Mom added some hot water to the tub and took my siblings into another room. As she left, she set a cane-backed chair near the door.

"You can prop this chair under the doorknob if you want to," she said without making eye contact.

As soon as they had left the room, I jumped up and secured the door, pulled all the curtains shut, and shyly removed my gown. I remember thinking Mom was my very best friend in the world that day. ⁊

My Chair-ished Friend

by Judy Eble Kiel McKain | *Andover, Ohio*

I TUGGED MY SISTER MONA'S TINY HAND as we followed Mamma that spring day in 1950. The chairs were painted ivory with red rings circling the beaded wood on the spokes of the chair backs. I spotted them on the side porch of the old farmhouse near Andover, Ohio, where the auction was being held. I glanced over my shoulder and saw Mamma a few steps behind. I pointed to the chairs—she saw our smiles and dancing eyes and nodded. She knew we were already planning all the ways we'd use those little chairs. I saw her open her purse to take inventory, and my heart sank. There never seemed to be money for extras.

"What do I hear for a pair of chairs?" the auctioneer asked. A skinny lady in an orange dress was first to bid. I tried to read Mamma's face, but she just nodded when the bidding was at seventy cents. I closed my eyes tightly and waited until I heard the auctioneer smack that gavel and say "SOLD, one dollar for the pair of chairs!" I opened my eyes, and Mona and I rushed forward to claim our prizes! We eagerly pulled the little chairs across the lawn, tucking them safely into our old Ford coupe.

When we arrived home, we dusted off those chairs and carried them across the gravel road to the abandoned milk parlor that served as our playhouse. The chairs made a wonderful addition to the milk-bucket stools and cardboard box tables. That spring and summer, we picked beautiful bouquets of Queen Ann's lace, hollyhocks, and wild mustard to decorate our house. Mamma painted our chairs bright pink and they looked terrific. We whiled away the hours with talent shows, tea parties, and playing house.

One summer day, I found the hollyhocks had fallen and blocked our playhouse door. I ran to the house and borrowed my brother's Boy Scout hatchet—his pride and joy. Days later, when the hatchet was missing, I confessed to Charles that I was the one who took it, and helped him search the high weeds. When he found it, the blade was already rusted.

With anger in his eyes, Charles yelled at me to stay away from his things, and then he drew that hatchet high and with two swift blows—*swack, swack*—laid two big ugly gashes into the seat of my precious chair.

In days to come, my chair and I sat outside the outhouse while Mona was inside. My chair boosted me to the countertop where I pushed sweet yellow peaches into the canning jars for Mamma, and helped me reach the high end of the clotheslines when the rain came quicker than my big sisters. My chair boosted me to just the right height to rest my skinny elbows on the fenders of Dad's jalopy. I could view the whole engine from that vantage point. I learned about points and plugs and all kinds of interesting things. When the mosquitoes got too bad in Dad's little shed, I'd take my chair indoors and pull up a seat to our TV with its snowy ten-inch screen and watch *Your Hit Parade*.

When our family decided to buy our grandfather's farm and move to Acme, Indiana, my older sisters were sad to leave Andover behind. But Charles, Mona, and I were sure it would be a fine adventure and were happy about getting to know our grandfather better. That summer, I sat on my chair on the front porch and waved at unfamiliar faces, and sat beneath the shady maple, too. We tended garden, walked to the country store for hard candy, and hugged Grandpa's neck a lot.

It was a raw November evening in 1955 when my brother yelled from the kitchen, "Dad, the house is on fire!" The first thing Dad did was survey the fire. Before beginning his fight against it, he ran with us to the neighbor's lane.

Bending down to peer into our faces, he said, "Daddy's got to get some water on this fire—now you stay right here—stay together and no matter what favorite things you think of—you mustn't go back in—do you understand me?" Nodding soberly we obeyed.

The flames were shooting high. Neighbors were gathering to help. I heard glass breaking. Then I saw Mr. Bevers come across the road toward us. He was holding a long pole, no—it was one of our stilts—and on the end of it was a small chair. My heart leapt! Was it my chair or was it Mona's? He deposited it near us and holding Mona's hand I rubbed my fingers across the seat. I felt the two deep hatchet marks—for the first time, they were beautiful!

But in months and years to come, I found little time for my chair and my bigger bottom didn't fit it well.

In the fall of 1968, my daughter, Susan, pulled that little chair next to my recliner, rolled up her tiny T-shirt, and gently pulled her baby doll to her chest to nurse as I nursed her baby sister, Liz. In another year and a half Liz dragged the chair to the kitchen and stood on tiptoes to lick beaters covered with chocolate. In yet another two years, daughter number three, Christine, tied her teddy bear to the chair and pushed it across the room. Ah the memories—oops—a broken leg—paint well worn—off to the attic went my precious chair. But twelve years later, on Mother's Day 1980, my chair wears a red ribbon. She's solid oak, minus pink paint, ivory paint, and three more layers of paint. She sports a new leg turned to match the other three, and this time she's valued at $50, not fifty cents. Her restoration was expensive but worth every penny. I wouldn't take $500 for her. She's a priceless treasure from my girlhood and that of my daughters. My grandchildren—all nine of them—line up to take turns sitting on my chair-ished friend.

The Time Capsule

by Leslie J. Wyatt | *Clinton, Missouri*

"AAAHHH! GEORGIA MAE! NO-NO! Give Mama her keys." My friend Cynthia pries her car keys from her toddler's hands seconds before they disappear into the heater vent of her Victorian-era house. "Yesterday it was a pencil," she said. "And before that—who knows?"

Yes, who knows? But some day—some long-into-the-future day—when her furnace decides to issue its much-overdue resignation, there will be a final *whump* from the dark and musty region under the century-old floor and the familiar, grumbly voice will refuse to speak.

My friend will call the repairman, then. I'm sure of that, because Missouri winters can be nagging and cold. So she'll call and he'll come, and of course he'll pronounce the old workhorse of a furnace deceased before going away to retrieve its successor. But on the day the repairman arrives with the new heating unit, Cynthia will cry.

How do I know that? Because I know that on the day the heater vents are disconnected from the old furnace, the repairman will uncover a time capsule, and my friend will take a journey back in time.

This will not be your typical cylinder or box containing a record of dates and history. On the contrary, seeing the light of day for the first time in years and years, an array of items will knock on memory's door: Three matchbox cars. Those would be from the time two-year-old Luke discovered the loose vent cover on the stair landing. Cynthia will see again his baby cheeks, his eyes wide in delight, his determination to hear that certain clattering, skittering sound as he casts yet another car into the black hole.

There will be pennies. Not riches by any measure except that of remembered days of delight—Georgia Mae's delight—as she crouched, diaper on heels, toddler-style, to drop those coins one by one before Mama could intervene.

My guess is that there will be paper records of past days as well. Maybe a drawing of a horse, signed by Hannah—who by then may very well be a mother herself, and Cynthia will remember the lawns her daughter mowed, the money saved, and the day Hannah bought her long-dreamed-of and prayed-for horse.

Surely there will be a couple of photos, perhaps one of Ruby, the silver pug puppy of Madeline's thirteen-year-old dreams. That picture will bring back in crystal clarity the afternoon Mark smuggled the puppy into the house in his backpack, just to surprise this daughter of his so she'd know she was special.

There'll be art by Emma Grace, items penned by Eli—these, too, will emerge from their dusty dwelling place, long after the children are grown and gone and no little bare feet pound across the hardwood floors.

Not realizing he's touching relics precious to baby days, childhood ways, and countless hours of motherhood, the furnace man will scrape them off into a box and deposit it in Cynthia's hand.

"It's no wonder that furnace burnt itself out, ma'am," he'll say. "With all this stuff sitting on top the air intake and outflow vents."

She'll smile and nod as she takes that box to a quiet place where she can laugh and cry in peace. Maybe she'll make herself some tea. She'll have time for that now—and no little hands will reach up to "share" her cup, for the days when the time capsule was in the making are behind her. They whizzed by in a whirlwind of diaper changing, late-night feedings, chauffeuring, and kids' homework.

But they were good years, sweet years, fleeting as the season of spring, poignant with the intensity of children. So she'll laugh. And she'll cry, because it will seem like just last week that she rescued her keys seconds before they joined the other treasures in the heater vent, or yesterday when she said to me, "We're building our own time capsule around here."

And so they are. I wonder what was added today. . . .

Be a part of
The Rocking Chair Reader *series* . . .

We hope you've enjoyed *Memories from the Attic* as much as we've enjoyed bringing it to you. It goes without saying that those who lived or live in small-town America have a story to tell that bears repeating, and we invite you to share yours with us for possible publication in future volumes of *The Rocking Chair Reader*.

When submitting to *The Rocking Chair Reader*, you may submit as many stories as you like. Please remember to include your name, address, phone number, and the name of the small town your story is written about.

Send all correspondence to *rockingchairreader@adamsmedia.com*. If e-mail is not available, please snail mail to:

The Rocking Chair Reader
Adams Media
57 Littlefield Street
Avon, Massachusetts 02322

Current guidelines can be found at *www.rockingchairreader.com*. Everyone has a story to tell, and we'd love to hear yours.

Contributors

Joyce A. Anthony ("Almost Heaven") was born in Pennsylvania and lives there today with her son, Shane. She is both a writer and a photographer. For more information regarding her work, please visit her Web site at: *http://bi-polarbears.com/Paws/night.php*.

Trish Ayers ("Angela's Hidden Treasure"), a twenty-year resident of Berea, Kentucky, has been writing since she could hold a pencil. Working on essays, poetry, short stories, novels, and especially plays has become a healing salve for her while facing a chronic illness. As a playwright, her works have been produced and staged in Kentucky, Seattle, Pennsylvania, and across the country, and in Japan.

Kim Ballard ("Open Windows") is a published author who writes fiction and nonfiction and is currently seeking agent representation for her most recently completed novel, *Birth Parents*. Two current projects include young adult fiction as well as a science fiction novel. Kim loves taking breaks from writing to walk on the beach near her home in Palm City, Florida.

Laverne Bardy-Pollak ("Clinging to the Past") writes a humorous column titled "Laverne's View," which has appeared in more than fifty New Jersey newspapers and has been picked up for syndication with

Senior Wire. Her work has been published in various anthologies and magazines. Laverne is currently working on two books: a memoir and a compilation of her columns.

Rollie Barton ("Church House Mouse"), raised in the Midwest—a Depression kid of World War II vintage—is the father of five, grandfather of fourteen, and great-grandfather of eight. Rollie served nearly six years in the military in rank from buck private to captain by the war's end. Based in Italy, he saw combat duty as a fighter pilot with the 15th Air Force in the weapon of choice, a P-51 Mustang. He met his girl, Irene, while stationed at Bakersfield, California. They were married after the war and lived happily ever after.

Sande Boritz Berger ("Reels of Love"), after nearly two decades as a scriptwriter and video/film producer, has returned to her first passion: writing both fiction and nonfiction full-time. Her work has been published in several anthologies, including *Aunties* and *A Cup of Comfort,* and in various small-press magazines and newspapers. Sande recently completed a first novel and is at work on a second.

Lanita Bradley Boyd ("Going, Going . . . Gone!") is a freelance writer in Fort Thomas, Kentucky. Her writing springs from many years of teaching, church ministries, and family experiences. She can be reached through her Web site at *www.lanitaboyd.com.*

Barbara Brady ("Strong Stuff" and "The Diploma"), a retired RN, lives in Topeka, Kansas, with her husband of almost fifty years. She enjoys church, sunflowers, books, and volunteer activities, but most of all, family and friends. Barbara is the author of *A Variety of Gifts, Smiling at the Future,* and *Seasoned with Salt.* Her work has been published in various markets.

Marcia E. Brown ("Putting Down Roots" and "When Pop-Pop Was a Pillar") of Austin, Texas, writes of her Depression-era childhood in Oklahoma and Arkansas to preserve family stories for her son and cousins. Since 1993, her work has appeared regularly in magazines, newspapers, and anthologies, including *The Rocking Chair Reader* and the *Cup of Comfort* series.

Guy Carrozzo ("The Ice Ball Machine") was born in Pennsylvania in 1932. His family moved to California in 1946. He graduated from high school, served four years in the U.S. Air Force, attended college, and was married. He served thirty years in education, five as a teacher and twenty-five as a principal. He has two adult children and four grandchildren.

Lisa Ciriello ("A Mother's Gift") is a freelance writer and baker. She lives in Warwick, New York, with her husband and pets.

Nan B. Clark ("Starting Life at the Top") and her husband, Tom, live in Beverly, Massachusetts, where they have shared an interest in the history of Boston's North Shore for more than three decades. Nan has also been involved for many years in The Society for the Preservation of New England Antiquities, first as an artisan teaching eighteenth-century japanning techniques and then as a tour guide in the society's forty-room mansion, Beauport, located on Gloucester Harbor.

Joan Clayton ("I Wouldn't Have Missed It for the World") is a retired educator who also has been the religion columnist for her local newspaper for eleven years. She has written eight books and has had over 500 articles published. Joan has appeared three times in *Who's Who Among America's Teachers* and was Woman of the Year 2003 in her town of Portales, New Mexico. She has been married to the love of her life for fifty-six years, and has three sons and six grandchildren.

Karen Commings ("Saving It for Good") is an award-winning writer and author of eight books on pet care. Karen, a former magazine columnist, was a contributing editor for *Cat Fancy* magazine and Pets.com. She writes regularly for *Cat Watch* and *Dog Watch*, the newsletters of the Cornell University School of Veterinary Science, and also writes short stories under a pen name.

Betty Davis ("Community Tub") was educated in Springfield, Missouri, and then moved to Houston, Texas, where she now lives. Betty's work has been published in magazines, including *Suddenly V; New Texas; Albany Review; Buffalo Spree;* and *Texas Poetry Calendar,* which she coedited.

Michele Deppe ("The Mystery Rider") holds a degree in nutrition and is a licensed cosmetologist. Her interests include fitness, reading, cooking, gardening, and riding horses in the classical discipline known as dressage. She resides in her hometown of Dayton, Ohio, with her artist husband, Tod, and a spoiled Shih Tzu puppy named Chloe. Michele has written articles on a variety of topics for publication in numerous magazines.

Betty Downs ("The Brass Bell") was raised on the prairies of North Dakota but has called the Black Hills of South Dakota home for the past fifty years, forty of which were spent moving through four states with her construction-roving husband. Now widowed, Betty is enjoying gardening and traveling, and is delighted to be published in *The Upper Room, Reminisce, A Cup of Comfort,* and the anthology *Crazy Woman Creek.* She has four sons and seven grandchildren who keep life interesting.

Sandy Williams Driver ("Dear Daddy") and her husband, Tim, live in Albertville, Alabama, where both were born and raised. They have three children: Josh, Jake, and Katie. Sandy has been a full-time writer for three years. Her stories have been included in several magazines, newspapers, and anthologies, including *The Rocking Chair Reader: Coming Home.*

Melinda Fausey ("Pelican Summer") has had work published in several magazines and anthologies as well as with Blue Mountain Arts. Recently, Melinda made the best decision of her life when she gave up a full-time career in radiology to be a stay-at-home mom for her three young children, and to devote time to her love of writing.

Leslie A. Friesen ("The Times They Aren't A-Changin'") is a single mother of four children and a professional Web designer. Her writing credits include magazine articles, several monthly newsletters, copy for numerous Web sites, technical software manuals, and a monthly column in her local newspaper. Currently, Leslie is writing an inspirational book tentatively titled "Escaping a Polyester and Vinyl World," and a preschool curriculum for homeschoolers entitled "A to Z: Play with Me." In addition, she owns and operates Scarlett Design, a small Web site design business, which can be found at: *www.scarlettdz9.com.*

Robert N. Going ("Honor Roll") is an aging baby-boomer attorney in Amsterdam, New York. Robert has been an assistant district attorney, assistant public defender, city court judge, family court judge, paperboy, rug cleaner, security guard, and snow cone man. He and his wife, Mary, have four children. For four weeks in 2001, Robert sliced bagels at Respite Center One at Ground Zero, NYC, as a Red Cross volunteer.

John R. Gugel ("The Trunk in the Attic") is a freelance author and minister on disability leave. His most recent book is titled *Cries of Faith, Songs of Hope: Prayers for the Times of Our Life.* He and his wife, Linda, have three grown children: Jeremy, Jessica, and Nathan.

Lynn R. Hartz ("Singing on the Front Porch") lives in Charleston, West Virginia. Her stories have appeared in *A Cup of Comfort for Christmas* and *Small Miracles for Families*. She has authored three books: *And Time Stood Still*, the story of the midwife who delivered the Christ Child; *Club Fed: Living in a Women's Prison;* and *Praise Him in Prison*.

M. DeLoris Henscheid ("The Talking Machine"), the sixth of eight consecutive generations of women in her family who have lived in Blackfoot, Idaho, is the mother of nine grown children. DeLoris received her B.A. in Early Childhood Education from Idaho State University, taught kindergarten for eight years, and since retirement has been active in the Idaho Writer's League, concentrating on stories of the women in her family.

Joyce McDonald Hoskins ("The Table Traveled Home") grew up in Clarksburg, West Virginia, and has been a longtime resident of Stuart, Florida. She is an antiques dealer and an author of two mystery novels. When not writing or looking for antiques, Joyce enjoys her pets and working in her flower gardens.

Roberta Beach Jacobson ("Sisters of Summer") is a freelance writer whose work has appeared in *McCall's, Capper's, Woman's Day, Natural Home, Transitions Abroad,* and *I Love Cats*. She makes her home on a remote Greek island and can be reached at *www.travelwriters.com/ Roberta*.

Jim James ("The Auction") published his first novel, *Paris, Wyoming,* in 2003. His writing also has appeared in several newspaper columns, and in his master's thesis and doctoral dissertation.

Lorna M. Kaine ("A Sign of Love") is a retired teacher, lab technician, and computer programmer. She has been published in various newspapers and magazines, including *Orlando Sentinel, Orlando Voice, Oviedo Voice, Feline Fables, Dogwood Tales,* and *Up Dare?*

Candy Killion ("Beach Patrol"), a freelance writer living near Fort Lauderdale, Florida, lived more than four decades in New Jersey—each move bringing her a little bit closer to the beach. Her work has appeared in numerous newspapers, magazines, greeting cards, and on the Net, as well as in the *They Lied!* humor anthology series.

Tony Lolli ("The Mountain Rises Again") is a freelance writer from East Burke in the Northeast Kingdom of Vermont. He also runs Get Lost: A Four Season Outdoor Guide Service, whose motto is "We (almost) always find our way back."

Grace Walker Looper ("A Precious Memory") is a former English teacher and library/media specialist with a master's degree in English and school librarianship. She has attended numerous writers' conferences and workshops, won writing contests, and has had her work accepted by various publications. She belongs to the Charlotte Writers Club, the South Carolina Writers Workshop, the Southeastern Writers Conference, and two critique groups.

Beverly Carol Lucey ("Home Away from Home") has had her work published in several anthologies as well as in *Portland Maine Magazine, Flint River Review, Moxie, Quality Women's Fiction* (UK), and in *Wild Strawberries.*

Helen Luecke ("The Perfect Place") lives in Amarillo, Texas, with her husband, Richard. She is cofounder of Inspirational Writers Alive! Amarillo chapter. She writes short stories, articles, and devotionals.

She has been published in several anthologies, *Mature Living*, and *Home Life*, as well as in other inspirational publications.

Gloria MacKay ("Out to Lunch") hosts a weekly radio program (on KSER). Her cookbook *Easy Cooking from Scratch* began as motherly advice to her four grown sons. Her most recent collection, *Throwing Sticks and Skipping Stones*, is available at dlsijpress.com, where she also appears in *The Insomniac Tales of Chaucer's Women*. Her work appears in two anthologies: *Forget Me Knots...from the Front Porch* and the *Don't Sweat Stories: Inspirational Anecdotes from Those Who've Learned How Not to Sweat It* from Hyperion.

Steven Manchester ("Letters from the Front") is the father of two sons. He also is the published author of *The Unexpected Storm: The Gulf War Legacy, Jacob Evans, A Father's Love*, and *At the Stroke of Midnight* as well as several books under the pseudonym Steven Herberts. His work has been showcased in such national literary journals as *Taproot Literary Review, American Poetry Review*, and *Fresh! Literary Magazine*. When not spending time with his sons, writing, teaching, or promoting his work, he speaks publicly to troubled children through the "Straight Ahead" Program.

Judy Eble Kiel McKain ("My Chair-ished Friend") is a survivor—like her chair-ished friend. She has raised three daughters, been widowed, survived cancer, and recently remarried. She is a freelance writer of devotional pieces and human interest stories. Judy currently lives in Jackson County, Indiana, near her childhood home, where she is active in church activities, serves as a Hospice volunteer, and entertains locally with her poems and stories.

Pat Capps Mehaffey ("A Gift from Mother"), an ex-banker, retired to a lake cabin where she enjoys birds, grandchildren, and writing. From the serenity of this location, Pat wrote and published two Christian meditation books, had several stories accepted in the *Cup of Comfort* series of books, and in 2003, won first place in a regional obituary-writing contest.

Alice A. Mendelsohn ("Gramma's Ring") has written poetry since she was a little girl. She is a member of Women Who Write and has discovered the enjoyment of creative nonfiction and personal essays. In recent years, Alice was privileged to have a bylined column in a local newspaper and more recently has had poems appear in local publications.

Lynn Ruth Miller ("The Laugh Took the Prize") writes a regular holiday column called "Thoughts While Walking the Dog" in *The Pacifica Tribune,* and has had her work published throughout the country. The author of four books and one audio CD, Lynn Ruth also is the hostess of two public access television programs: Channel 26 in Pacifica: "What's Hot Between the Covers" (book reviews and interviews in the arts) and "Paint with Lynn," a hands-on creative arts series. Recently, Lynn Ruth has begun a new career in stand-up comedy and appears throughout the Bay Area on a regular basis.

Lad Moore ("The Penny Block"), a former corporate executive, has returned to his roots in east Texas. His writings have been published more than 400 times in print and on the Web, including two short-story collections at *BeWrite Books.* He has received several writing awards and credits, which include appearances in *Carolina Country, Amarillo Bay, Pittsburgh Quarterly,* and in various anthologies. Visit Lad's Web site at *http://ladmoore.homestead.com/home.html.*

David E. Morton ("Sunshine") is a freelance writer living in Minnesota. David, a classical music fan—especially of Mozart—has written about a "trademark phrase," often deeply embedded, found primarily in Mozart's music. When David is not writing, reading, or listening to Mozart, he dons his plastic pocket protector and relaxes with his old-computer simulators for a nostalgic trip down memory lane, something he says he actually enjoys.

Thelma Vaughan Mueller ("Whistle Stop in Irondale") was born in Birmingham, Alabama, in 1929. She lived in Europe and Philadelphia for a number of years, then returned to Alabama, where she served on the faculty of the Department of Psychiatry, University of Alabama Medical School, and later on the graduate faculty of the School of Social Work, University of Alabama, in Tuscaloosa. A collection of her short stories appears in *Perspectives*.

Vanessa K. Mullins ("Reclining Memories") lives with her husband and three children in Michigan. She has published two novels and compiled one anthology. She is cofounder of the Southeast Michigan Writer's Association.

Emmy Lou Nefske ("The Undiscovered Classic") was born and raised in northern Michigan. She has lived in eight different cities across the state, from Sault Ste. Marie to Ypsilanti, including Mackinac Island. An aspiring novelist, Emmy is currently a high school math teacher in Hamtramck, Michigan.

Carol Nyman ("Moving On") now lives in Summerville, South Carolina, and is a member of SC Writers Group. Another one of her stories can be found in *The Rocking Chair Reader: Coming Home*.

Linda Kaullen Perkins ("The Jewelry Box"), freelance writer and novelist, has had articles published in several local newspapers and currently contributes a monthly selection of short stories to *Party*

Line, a local magazine. After retiring in 2001 after thirty-one years as an elementary teacher, Linda completed a 70,000-word historical manuscript. She is a member of Heartland Romance Authors, Romance Writers of America, and a weekly critique group.

Charles Perry ("The Spirit of the Journey") is a freelance photographer and writer. His photographs of the Belen, New Mexico, wild horses snowballed into statewide recognition of the horses and their plight, and garnered national interest, including several National Geographic television programs in 2001. As an animal lover and conservationist, Charles has belonged to many animal rights organizations. Through his work, he hopes others will see the value of all wild animals and learn to understand the historic value of North America's wild horses.

Connie Koopman Pettersen ("Grandma's House") is a contributing author in *Stories for a Soldier's Heart, A Christian Reader, Cricket* magazine group, *Aglow, War Cry, Witness, Lutheran Woman Today,* and *Woman's Touch.*

Cheryl Pierson ("Penny Memories") lives in Oklahoma City with her husband and two children. Cheryl, a freelance writer and novelist, is currently working on her third romance novel and is co-owner of FabKat Editorial Services, where she teaches workshops and weekly writing classes as well as edits manuscripts for other authors.

Penny Porter ("Crossing Bridges"), married to Bill Porter, a retired cattle rancher, is the mother of six, grandmother of eight, and great-grandmother of one. She has always been in love with life and family. Penny, the author of five books, currently is president of the Society of Southwestern Authors. Her work has been published in a wide range of magazines, including *Reader's Digest, Arizona Highways, Guideposts, Catholic Digest,* and several anthologies.

Carbon Rains ("Single Shot .22") grew up on a small farm near Oklahoma City. Today, she lives in Oklahoma City and works as an RN. On special occasions, she gets together with family to enjoy re-telling the stories passed down by their parents (all of whom have since passed on).

Marilyn Rodriguez ("The Rocking Horse") was born in 1942, grew up in a small town, and raised her son in the same small town. When her son was six, they moved to a larger city. Marilyn's grandchildren love the stories she writes for them, and she enjoys finally having the time to study writing and work on her novels.

Gin Rowledge ("My Mother's Mirror") grew up in hilly Connecticut country with lots of time to read and appreciate sky, clouds, and wildflowers. She graduated in 1953, and moved to Florida in 1971, where she is a hearing instrument specialist. Virginia finds it gratifying to help people to hear the sounds of life. Writing is her passion.

Al Serradell ("The Coin"), a Los Angeles native, is a veteran writing instructor in the Oklahoma City area. A professional journalist, he has worked for newspapers in Oklahoma (*The Journal Record, The Guthrie News Leader*) and Colorado (*The Rocky Mountain News*), and co-owns an editorial business, FabKat Editorial Services.

Annette H. Sharp ("Return to Irish Town") is the eldest of Kellett and Joan Hathorn's seven children. Through her rich heritage of family members who immigrated to the United States, Annette shares some of the family's treasures.

Merry Simmons ("Skipping Stones"), a real estate broker who happily sells others a piece of small-town life, lives in Wilson, North

Carolina. She's married to her high school sweetheart. Together, they have one grown son and two incredible grandsons.

Shauna Smith-Duty ("Pickled Beets") homeschools her two children in Roanoke, Texas. She loves to bring joy to her readers through light-hearted humor and biographical articles.

Cheryl D. Stauffer ("Buttons and Clover"), a former music teacher from Atlanta, lives with her husband in France, where they work as musicians in a church just outside of Lyon. In addition to caring for her three children, Cheryl loves to read, draw, write, and spend time with her family. She loves to write about her childhood, being a parent, and living abroad. Visit their Web site at: *http://stauffermission. homestead.com.*

Kelly L. Stone ("The House in the Picture") is a poet, essayist, and novelist. Her first novel, *Between Truth and Consequence,* is currently seeking a publisher. Kelly is also an animal welfare activist working to end the homeless pet problem by promoting spay/neuter. Visit her online at *www.kellylstone.com.*

Gayle Sorensen Stringer ("A Precious Rose") resides in a big city today but grew up on a dairy farm near the small southwestern Minnesota community of Tyler. A teacher and writer, Gayle is the mother of three children, and is eternally grateful for her small-town roots. She feels fortunate to have spent her childhood in a community where everyone knew her name—and everyone cared.

Lester Tucker ("Grandma's Boat") was born in 1956 in Tifton, Georgia. He and his wife, Sandra, have been married for twenty-five years. Lester has been writing since elementary school and has a passion for the literary arts. He enjoys retirement and spending time with his family.

Ray Weaver ("The Louisville Slugger") is a published singer/songwriter. Originally from the United States, Ray now lives and works in Denmark.

Barbara Wild ("Gettin' from Here to There") spent a very happy early childhood in the town of Frisco and on a small farm just outside of town. Today, Barbara is married with two children and twelve grandchildren. She is employed as a nurse and continues a career as a writer and member of Wyoming Writers, INC.

Genevieve Williams ("Home Delivery") was born in a houseboat on the Delaware River. In 1995, after living in Pennsylvania, West Virginia, and Miami, Florida, she and her husband, Jim, moved to the Atlanta area. Genevieve is now retired and busily writing stories while enjoying life in Georgia.

Linda C. Wisniewski ("A Ride on Grandma's Glider") is a former librarian who lives with her family in Bucks County, Pennsylvania, where she writes for a weekly newspaper. Linda also teaches a memoirs class at Bucks County Community College and facilitates a women's spiritual writing group at her church. Her work has been published in various magazines.

Leslie J. Wyatt ("The Time Capsule") is a freelance writer for children and adults, with more than fifty articles and stories in publication. Her work appears in various anthologies, including *A Cup of Comfort for Courage*, *My Heart's First Steps*, and *Yahweh Sisterhood*. Her first middle-grade historical novel is under contract. Leslie conducts writing workshops and is a featured conference speaker at select workshops. She and her husband have been blessed with six children and live in an 1880s Victorian farmhouse in rural Missouri.

Kristine Ziemnik ("As the Parade Passes By") lives with her husband, Joseph, in lovely, historic Chippewa Lake, Ohio. She owns a home-based craft business called Kristine's Kreations. Writing stories is another of her creative outlets, and she plans to write a book someday.

About the Editor

HELEN KAY POLASKI has always believed in magic, especially the kind that keeps marriages together, binds siblings and friends, and ties the concept of home close to the heart. She is the seventh child in a family of sixteen children and hails from a small town in northern Michigan, near the shores of Lake Huron, where she met and married her high school sweetheart.

After seventeen years as a newspaper reporter/photographer and editor, she left her full-time job to follow her dream of becoming a book author. In the past four years, she has worn many hats, including book author, book editor, storyteller, essayist, journalist, poet, book and movie reviewer, songwriter, and copresident of the Southeast Michigan Writers' Association. When not on the computer, she is busy exploring the world with her husband and three children, and is pleased to say most trips still take her back to Metz, Michigan, where she was born and raised, and where the magic is strongest.